This series offers the concerned reader basic guidelines and *practical* applications of religion for today's world. Although decidedly Christian in focus and emphasis, the series embraces all denominations and modes of Bible-based belief relevant to our lives today. All volumes in the Steeple series are originals, freshly written to provide a fresh perspective on current—and yet timeless—human dilemmas. This is a series for our times. Among the books:

How to Read the Bible
James Fischer

How to Live Your Faith
L. Perry Wilbur

A Spiritual Handbook for Women
Dandi Daley Knorr

Temptation: How Christians Can Deal with It
Frances Carroll

*With God on Your Side: A Guide to Finding
Self-Worth Through Total Faith*
Doug Manning

A Daily Key for Today's Christians: 365 Key Texts of the New Testament
William E. Bowles

Walking in the Garden: Inner Peace from the Flowers of God
Paula Connor

How to Bring Up Children in the Catholic Faith
Carol and David Powell

*Sex in the Bible: An Introduction to
What the Scriptures Teach Us About Sexuality*
Michael R. Cosby

*How to Talk with God Every Day of the Year:
A Book of Devotions for Twelve Positive Months*
Frances Hunter

*God's Conditions for Prosperity:
How to Earn the Rewards of Christian Living*
Charles Hunter

Pilgrimages: A Guide to the Holy Places of Europe for Today's Traveler
Paul Lambourne Higgins

*Journey into the Light: Lessons of Pain and Joy
to Renew Your Energy and Strengthen Your Faith*
Dorris Blough Murdock

God and Nature

A Book of Devotions for Christians Who Love Wildlife

NORMA J. PERSSON

A SPECTRUM BOOK

PRENTICE-HALL, INC., Englewood Cliffs, New Jersey 07632

Library of Congress Cataloging in Publication Data

Persson, Norma J.
   God and nature.

   (Steeple Books)
   "A Spectrum Book."
   Bibliography: p.
   Includes indexes.
   1. Animals—Religious aspects—Christianity—Prayer-books and devotions—English.   I. Title.   I. Series.
   BV4596.A54P47 1984   231.7'65   83-24767
   ISBN 0-13-357567-5
   ISBN 0-13-357559-4 (pbk.)

I dedicate this book to my mother, Carrie Nickeson, who at eighty-one years young has been my loving and honest "sounding board" during the writing.

This book is available at a special discount when ordered in bulk quantities. Contact Prentice-Hall, Inc., General Publishing Division, Special Sales, Englewood Cliffs, New Jersey 07632.

© 1984 by Prentice-Hall, Inc., Englewood Cliffs, New Jersey 07632
A SPECTRUM BOOK

All rights reserved. No part of this book may be reproduced in any form or by any means without permission in writing from the publisher.
10 9 8 7 6 5 4 3 2 1
Printed in the United States of America

Editorial/production supervision by Jane Zalenski
Cover design by Hal Siegel
Manufacturing buyer: Doreen Cavallo

All scripture passages are taken from *The Living Bible* (Wheaton, Illinois: Tyndale House Publishers, 1971).

ISBN 0-13-357567-5

ISBN 0-13-357559-4 {PBK.}

PRENTICE-HALL INTERNATIONAL, INC., *London*
PRENTICE-HALL OF AUSTRALIA PTY. LIMITD, *Sydney*
PRENTICE-HALL CANADA INC., *Toronto*
PRENTICE-HALL OF INDIA PRIVATE LIMITED, *New Delhi*
PRENTICE-HALL OF JAPAN, INC., *Tokyo*
PRENTICE-HALL OF SOUTHEAST ASIA PTE. LTD., *Singapore*
WHITEHALL BOOKS LIMITED, *WELLINGTON, New Zealand*
EDITORA PRENTICE-HALL DOBRASIL, LTDA., *Rio de Janeiro*

Contents

FAITH/ 1

LOVE/ 49

PERFORMANCE/ 65
 Ability/ 67
 Action/ 82

PRAISE/ 100

PERSEVERANCE/ 125

SELF-CONTROL/ 151

STEWARDSHIP/ 181

BIBLIOGRAPHY/ 223

SUBJECT INDEX/ 225

SCRIPTURE INDEX/ 227

Foreword

"Woe unto them that join house to house, that lay field to field, till there be no place that they may be placed alone in the midst of the earth." Isaiah 5:8.

Has there ever been a stronger call to care for the Earth? Has there ever been a better reason to care for the natural environment? Does any environmental organization have a stronger statement of philosophy than the church?

Yet the largest of the environmental groups, the church, is often, too quiet. The Bible is a strong book of philosophy and belief, but it is also a strong statement of obligation. What other group claims the inheritance of the Earth? Not ownership, although that too is often claimed, but inheritance, a legacy that is timeless and which should be passed as an heirloom, with care and preservation of its beauty and significance, from generation to generation.

"The land shall not be sold forever: for the land is mine: for ye are strangers and sojourners with me." Leviticus 25:23.

Like the American Indian, the Christian should say, "The land does not belong to me, but, rather, I belong to the land." Hypocrisy, some say, but Deuteronomy 10:14 states that "the heaven and the heaven of heavens is the Lord's thy God, the earth also, with all that therein is."

The Christian must be concerned when the Bible and the church are used as scapegoats for exploitation and greed. Can we really see God justifying the consumption of all our resources? Do we really believe God has created a great race for us in which we try to use up all of our resources before the second coming?

Or can we picture that the availability of resources is just one of the temptations of the wilderness that Christ symbolically fought and, in fact, we ought to seek the true values of the wilderness?

"He carried me away in the spirit into the wilderness." Revelation 17:3.

The Indians of the Southwest speak of beauty as being the essence of God. Their greetings are to "go in beauty." Can we feel otherwise when God has proclaimed, "it is good."

Wilderness, the preservation of beauty, and the love of the Earth are not just issues of politics and environment. They are the core of all of our beliefs. The Earth is our one common bond between all peoples.

The Indian, Black Elk, speaks of circles in describing the lifestyle of the Sioux Indian and their relation to the land. He sees the natural cycles reflected in people, if people are to prosper. The Christian has the same need to understand and protect our ecology.

The church has long been a user of the environment for retreats, youth camps, and inspirational settings, but for too long too many of our Christian programs have used without seeing. The church has been too much a part of society following the trends of architecture, finance, and social conscience. The wilderness, however, has long been a place for renewal of the spirit.

It is time for Christians to look back to the land, to relate to the Earth. The devotions in this book look for lessons in the world of nature—in the book of Isaiah the same kind of images were used.

                Michael Link, Director
                Northwoods Audubon Center, Minnesota

Preface

This book has a twofold purpose. The first and foremost is to point out the correlation between God and His creations. As we study the world of living creatures, we increasingly realize the wonderful plan behind all nature. There is no way that this plan could have been put into effect by mere chance. Each individual animal—each bird, fish, and insect—has been provided with the necessities for living, and each life intermingles with the others.

We can indeed take nature as a study-guide for life. Every creature has a lesson to share with us. In these pages I have done my best to point out some of these lessons in the hope that the reader will find them an inspirational help in his or her Bible studies and devotional times. The book is written to be used by adults, young people, and children.

The second purpose of the book is to convey information to you about our "neighbors," the many creatures with whom we share our world. It is my hope that when you complete the book, you will be more cognizant of their contributions and more aware of their needs than you are at this moment. If then you are moved to simply build a birdhouse or to scatter seed in the winter, or if you just become more watchful of wild creatures as you travel on the highways, these pages will have met their mark.

There is nothing more precious than the times we share the Lord and His Gospel with others, but the next thing we must do is to share His creations. In writing this manuscript, I have delighted in the content. I find myself much more aware than when I began of what is going on around me, whether it is the flight of a bird in the back yard or the journey of a tiny ant struggling with a gigantic load, pushing and pulling its way across the sidewalk.

Some of the best examples we have in life come from these creatures, large and small. We see the building ability of the little field mouse, the wisdom of the fox, the ambition of the beaver. There is no end, it seems—the unselfishness of the honey ant, the cooperation of the bitterling and the mussel. We have God's Word, the Bible, but He also gives us living lessons everywhere we look.

In the final analysis, these creatures must depend on man for their existence. It is man who destroys the timber, dams the rivers, and contaminates the waters that God's creations need for life itself.

Life—any life—is precious and needs to be protected. Of course death is included in the scheme of things, death does not mean wanton, needless destruction. Let us show compassion to *all* living things when compassion is called for. When animals are used by man as God intended, for food, clothing, and so on, let it be done in a humane manner, with wisdom instead of waste.

I pray that you will gain from reading this book as I have gained from writing it. I hope that it will bring you closer to God and to His creations so that you might see Him more clearly each day in the living world around you.

1
Faith

ROMANS 6:23 For the wages of sin is death, but the free gift of God is eternal life through Jesus Christ our Lord.

THE AYE-AYE

In far-off Madagascar
Lives a creature strange and rare—
He's only the size of a house cat,
With a coat of thick, dark hair.

His bushy tail is very long,
His naked ears erect.
The aye-aye's eyes are very large—
He's worthy of respect.

It took a while to classify
This shy creature with gnawing teeth.
At first it was thought to be a squirrel,
But he has a primate's hands and feet.

The Madagascan people
Regard the aye-aye with dread.
Their legends say that if you touch one,
You will soon be dead.

Since the aye-ayes are nocturnal, they are seldom seen by man. They live in the forests or mangrove and bamboo thickets. They are very rare, and steps are being taken to protect them from extinction. While this strange creature is a distant cousin of the lemur, it has no really close relatives. The Malagasy truly believe that to touch such an animal means death, and they are very fearful of aye-ayes. As humans, we too were afraid of death—and then Jesus came! Praise the Lord, we do not have to be afraid anymore. God has given us the promise of eternal life through His Son, Jesus Christ.

Dear Heavenly Father, thank You for this matchless gift—the gift of Your Son. I know that He died on the cross for me and is now with You in Glory. Help my faith to increase, Lord, and my doubts to disappear. I need have no fear of death, for death is a beginning—not an end.

DEUTERONOMY 32:11 He spreads his wings over them, even as an eagle overspreads her young. She carries them upon her wings—as does the Lord his people!

THE BALD EAGLE

The mighty soaring bald eagle
Shows us majesty.
He's the emblem of our country
And delights in flying free.

His profile—up to three feet long—
Eight feet from wing to wing;
With snow-white head and tailfeathers,
He is a regal thing.

He mates for life and raises chicks
With faithful love and care.
Bald eagles are model parents,
And equally they share.

The bald eagle is an unforgettable sight and one not often seen. In many parts of its range, it is becoming rare as time goes on. In some areas, however, it is making a slow but promising comeback. These regal birds are excellent parents, caring tenderly for their young. As the eagle spreads her wings over the nest, protecting her young chicks, so God spreads His wings of love over us, His children. As the eagles feed their young, so He feeds us with His Word as He draws us closer to Him through prayer.

Dear Lord, just as the mighty eagle denotes freedom, so You denote freedom for me—freedom from worry and freedom from sin. I know that I am safe in the shadow of Your wings, and I praise You, Lord, for all of Your many blessings.

MATTHEW 14:29b,30 So Peter went over the side of the boat and walked on the water toward Jesus. But when he looked around at the high waves, he was terrified and began to sink. "Save me, Lord!" he shouted.

THE BASILISK LIZARD

The basilisk lizard makes his home
In Central America and Mexico.
He lives along the riverbanks,
Close to the water's flow.

He is a slender lizard
With long, slim toes and tail.
Some species are adorned with crests,
But usually just the male.

This creature has the ability
to run across a stream
On the surface of the water
Until he loses steam!

Basilisk lizards have a fringe of scales along their rear toes that provide support as they dash over the surface of the water. If they slacken speed, however, they begin to sink, and then they must swim in the conventional manner. They are able to escape predators in this way, as well as to acquire insects for food. We are told in the Scriptures that Peter went out on the water to meet Jesus and was doing fine—until he took his eyes off his Master. As he lost the "speed of faith," he began sinking like the basilisk. If we keep our eyes on Jesus, we will stay afloat and be safe. Our faith will protect us from predators and feed us through the Word. Let us truly "keep the faith!"

Dear Lord, I pray that my eyes might be ever fixed on You and that my faith might not falter but grow ever stronger. Thank You, Lord, for holding me up when by myself I would sink in the waves of life.

ACTS 2:33 And now he [Jesus] sits on the throne of highest honor in heaven, next to God. And just as promised, the Father gave him the authority to send the Holy Spirit—with the results you are seeing and hearing today.

THE BELLBIRD

The metallic ringing of his song
Gives the bellbird his pretty name.
There are several species,
And they all sound much the same.

Few people view the crested one—
He's secretive as can be.
You may hear his bell-like tones
And search for him diligently.

He keeps a supply of food on hand,
And he may fill his nest
With living caterpillars or worms,
Whichever he likes best.

He's found in far Australia,
New Zealand—South America too.
He is a real ventriloquist,
Though he usually hides from view.

When the bellbird sings, it is difficult to find its position for its song seems to come from different places—first from faraway, then nearer, then far again. The country people in Australia put bells on their horses, and often they confuse the bell tones with the bellbird's song. They hear the song, but since the bird is so seldom seen, they forget that the song could be coming from it. We cannot see the Holy Spirit, and sometimes we forget to listen for Him. Let us keep our communication lines open that we might discern between the Holy Spirit and self—between what we should do and what we want to do.

Dear Lord, although I cannot see You physically, I feel Your Presence in my heart and in my life. Help me to remember always that You promised to be my constant companion—and that You never break a promise!

JOHN 3:16 For God loved the world so much that he gave his only Son so that anyone who believes in him shall not perish but have eternal life.

THE CHAMBERED NAUTILUS

A cousin of the octopus,
The chambered nautilus dwells
Hundreds of feet beneath the sea
In the most amazing shells.

He is of spiral beauty,
With tiny chambers round.
He's as old as civilization,
And very seldom found.

The creature travels backwards.
You mostly see the shell,
And nineteen pairs of tentacles
Around the mouth as well.

The ancients used this symbol
To depict eternity.
Around, around forever—
No start—no end, you see.

The chambered nautilus is enveloped in a spiral shell of individual chambers. As the creature grows, chambers are added. It is through these chambers that direction and speed are controlled. How simple the principle, yet how complex! The nautilus depicts the eternal life that God holds out to us—a life with Jesus Christ forever, growing in Him as the chambered nautilus grows within its shell.

Dear Heavenly Father, I pray that I may accept the gift that Jesus extends and that I might live my life trusting and obeying in His Word. The spiral shell of the chambered nautilus will serve as a reminder to me of our eternal life in Christ.

PSALMS 136:23,24 He remembered our utter weakness, for his lovingkindness continues forever. And saved us from our foes, for his lovingkindness continues forever.

THE CLICK BEETLE

The click beetle has a unique skill
To protect himself from attack,
For he can spring straight in the air
If he tumbles on his back.

Most beetles are rendered helpless
In such a sorry state,
But not this little "skipjack"—
He jumps e'er it's too late!

As he jumps, you'll hear a click—
It's just the way he's made.
God has cared for His creations
From the time the earth was laid.

God uses unique methods to give His creations protection from harm. With just a single speedy movement, the click beetle snaps the joint between the first and second segments of the thorax and sends itself leaping into the air, to land on its feet this time. God knows our weaknesses and compensates for them so that we too can "land on our feet." Sometimes we become discouraged and feel that all is lost, but the Lord is always there to pick us up and give us what we need to forge ahead again. Truly, His lovingkindness does continue forever, and we praise Him for that!

Dear Father in Heaven, I thank You and praise You for all You have provided me with. Not just the physical things, Lord, but all the many spiritual blessings. You know what I need before I even need it, and You compensate for my many weaknesses. I thank You, Lord, that You help me "land on my feet," and I pray that I may always lay my trust in the foundation of Your love.

PSALMS 54:4 But God is my helper. He is a friend of mine!

THE CLOWNFISH

The clownfish isn't very big,
But bright as bright can be!
He comes in different colors
And so, his name, you see.

He's easy prey when found alone,
But God gave him a place
Where he can be protected
From the constant chase.

He hides among the anemones
On the ocean floor.
They will protect the clownfish.
How could he ask for more?

The clownfish and the sea anemones are truly "strange bedfellows." The sea anemones have thousands of stinging cells in their tentacles, yet they never harm the clownfish as it weaves in and out among these arms. It hides in the anemone's mouth, with only its head sticking out, ducking completely inside the anemone when a predator comes within reach, and yet even there it remains safe and unharmed. Man has yet to discover what the anemone's benefit from this relationship is. But just as God has provided a safe place for the little clownfish, so He has provided a safe place for us—in His arms. He is always our helper, always our friend. If He so protects the brightly colored little fish, how can we have any doubts of His protection of us? What a wonderful provider He is!

Dear Heavenly Father, what a wonder You are! Your creations are perfect, my Lord, and all work together for good, just as You said. Help me to remember that all I am and all I have are because of You. You are always there to give help when I need it, and I cherish Your friendship. I pray that I might always be pleasing to You, but I know that You, as my friend, also understand when I fail. Praise You for Your great understanding and love.

PSALMS 119:68 You are good and do only good; make me follow your lead.

THE CROSSBILL

This bird got his name for a reason—
His mandibles are crossed.
He picks the seeds from conifer cones.
If they fall on the ground, they're lost.

He has large feet to grip the cones,
And is adept at climbing trees.
He can jump from branch to branch,
Picking cones to extract the seeds.

He migrates where the food is,
Living on the crop.
He may stay an entire year,
Then move to another stop.

The three species of crossbills in Europe have different bill sizes and feed on different kinds of cones. They all belong to the finch family, which raises its young entirely on seeds. In all three species, the males are brick red, with brown wings and tail, and the females and young have a green cast. Their unique bills are custom-made for acquiring their food. They follow their God-given instincts without hesitation, traveling from crop to crop. They are like sheep following a shepherd. We too have a Shepherd. God is good, and if we follow His leading, we have nothing to fear—unless we jumble the communication lines and let self get in the way. His plans for us are simple. The Gospel message is simple. Let us just take it as it is and obey, with complete trust in His Word.

Lord, help me to accept the truth, simple and sweet as it is. You loved me enough to die for me. You are good and do only good. Help me to follow Your lead without question or regret.

PROVERBS 14:26 Reverence for God gives a man deep strength; his children have a place of refuge and security.

THE DEER
(Mother and Fawn)

Her soft nose quivers
And she sighs—
You see the pain
In her bright eyes.

She struggles
In the misty dawn,
Giving birth
To her tiny fawn.

The quivering legs
Try hard to stand—
A soft, sweet cry
Of child demand.

A picture of nature
At its best—
Of love and motherhood
Put to the test.

Just as the beautiful doe feeds her tiny fawn, giving it sustenance, so does God watch over us, His children. As that fawn fully depends on its mother for survival, so we also fully depend on our Heavenly Father. Being a faithful Christian is not always easy. Our legs may buckle under the weight from time to time, but He is there to lift us up and to help us stand—to take our load when it gets too heavy. When we thirst, He gives us Living Water, and when we hunger, He feeds us through His Word. Praise the Lord, the great provider!

Dear Father in Heaven, please help me to learn to lean on You. I must stop trying to do everything on my own. I love and praise You for Your great love and concern for my life. Teach me to live it more and more for You, Who have given so abundantly to me.

PROVERBS 12:21 No real harm befalls the good, but there is constant trouble for the wicked.

THE DORMOUSE

The dormice, in their way of life,
And in the way they look,
Bridge the gap between mouse and squirrel—
A rather comfortable nook!

There are several species known,
And they are small, like mice.
Most of them have squirrel-like tails,
That are bushy and quite nice.

Their fur is soft and very dense—
Their color brown or gray.
Most of the dormice are nocturnal,
And rest throughout the day.

These little creatures are excellent climbers and live in trees and shrubs. They have long, flexible toes and can move over the slenderest branches with ease. They hibernate in the winter, and their mortality rate is low, as is their reproductive rate. With the large eyes of most nocturnal animals, they are unobtrusive little creatures who pretty much mind their own business, accomplishing what they need to do quietly and efficiently. We should strive to do the same! God equips the dormouse for survival, and He promises to keep us safe when we heed His Word. "No real harm befalls the good," He says. This is sometimes difficult to understand when we look around and see what is happening to God's children and what has befallen them in the past. We must stop and think on this, though. What is "real harm"? The only real harm to us is to the soul, and truly God keeps His promise and protects us from real harm. We are safe in the Spirit, and nothing can change that unless we ourselves turn away from God. What a glorious thought—we are eternally safe in the bosom of Christ!

Dear Heavenly Father, I am invincible through Your Son. Praise You for that, Lord. This body may be destroyed, but my soul will live forever because of Calvary. Help me bring this news to others, that they may claim the same promise.

PSALMS 104:24 O Lord, what a variety you have made! And in wisdom you have made them all! The earth is full of your riches.

THE FIELD MOUSE

Let us give all credit now
Where credit should be due.
Take the lowly field mouse,
An intelligent mammal, true.

Though often thought of with disdain
By disrespectful men,
This little animal is worth
Looking at again.

For the mouse is a master builder,
And researchers have found
No one can beat the home he builds
Protected under ground.

He uses the principle of the arch,
And builds his cities strong.
He makes use of ventilation,
And makes his tunnels long.

When the snow and ice appear,
They only serve to show
How strong his little fortress is
Beneath the ice and snow.

Truly, God has equipped this insignificant little creature with everything it needs for survival. A prolific bearer of offspring, it could probably survive by mere numbers, but since it has many predators, God has equipped it with a good ability to protect itself. If God does so much for the lowly little field mouse, how can we ever doubt His love and care for us?

Dear Lord in Heaven, I love You and praise You. As I see more and more of Your workings in the world of nature, my awe of You increases. Help me to use all You have given me, and continue to give me, to be the best that I can be, for Your Glory.

PSALMS 48:14 For this great God is our God forever and ever. He will be our guide until we die.

THE GOOSE

A graceful "vee" against the sky—
It's fall again—the geese fly high.
They're flying south, where warm winds blow,
Away from frosty ice and snow.

How do they know just when to fly?
How do they know just where and why?
Because our God takes care of all—
All earth is His—they hear His call.

If He will guide the lowly geese,
Then we should know He will not cease
From guiding us our whole life through,
If we have faith and ask Him to.

What a beautiful sight! The geese fly high, honking as they go—seemingly excited about their long trip in the autumn of the year. Occasionally they tire and swoop down on a lake to rest and feed. Then off they go again, in perfect symmetry. Truly they are poetry in motion. Just as the geese have the built-in knowledge that saves them from winter's harm, so we have the built-in knowledge of our Creator. Let us "let go and let God lead" as the geese do, fully trusting in His direction. As He leads the geese to safety, so He will lead us to Heaven's shore.

Dear Lord, give me the faith and ability to trust and obey as the beautiful geese do. Help me to follow Your leading with complete trust; to go where You guide, even if I do not understand the reasons. Help me to follow without question and to do as You would have me do.

JOHN 5:28,29 Don't be so surprised! Indeed the time is coming when all the dead in their graves shall hear the voice of God's Son, and shall rise again—those who have done good, to eternal life; and those who have continued in evil, to judgment.

THE HATCHET FISH

*In South American waters
A small freshwater fish is found.
Called the hatchet fish, he flies,
And his fins make a buzzing sound.*

*His name comes from the slim body,
The deep chest, and the tail.
He does resemble a hatchet
As over the water he sails.*

*He rarely exceeds four inches in length,
And makes a dash before taking to the air.
Once aloft, he can't change direction,
But his flapping fins get him there!*

The little freshwater hatchet fish is quite capable of flight. The pectoral fins can be flapped in the air, and it is this flapping that makes a strange, buzzing sound. There are several species, including the marbled hatchet fish, the black-winged hatchet fish, and the silver hatchet fish. Just as this little aquatic creature rises into the air, we also shall rise and meet Him Who has promised to never let us fall back into the pond but to live with Him forever and ever. What a future for us! When everything else seems to be falling around us, we have His precious promise—and there is nothing to fear.

Dear Heavenly Father, I love You and praise You for Your many blessings. Help me to be ready to meet You—along with my brothers and sisters in Christ—when the promised time comes.

MATTHEW 6:31-33 So don't worry at all about having enough food and clothing. Why be like the heathen? For they take pride in all these things and are deeply concerned about them. But your heavenly Father already knows perfectly well that you need them, and he will give them to you if you give him first place in your life and live as he wants you to.

THE HERMIT CRAB

If you've ever seen a hermit crab,
You know he has no shell.
His body's vulnerable and soft,
So he must find a place to dwell.

Basically, he's like a lobster,
Only smaller and modified.
He hunts until he finds a shell
That he can live inside.

He clings to his new home so hard
You cannot pry him out.
The shell becomes a part of the crab,
While he, like a snail, moves about.

The hermit crab has four pairs of walking legs. The two back pairs are modified and used as struts against the inner walls of the adopted shell. It also has well-developed pincers that it uses for opening barnacles and tube worms for food. Another way it collects food is by brushing surfaces with its mouth parts. Although the hermit crab has no shell of its own, God provides for one. He takes care of all His creations, and most especially does He take care of us, His children. We have no cause to worry or fret over our needs. If we are living in God's will, our needs will be amply provided for.

Dear Heavenly Father, thank You so much for Your love and care. I pray that I may never forget the many wondrous things You have done and continue to do for me. Help me to live my life for Your Glory.

HEBREWS 12:2 Keep your eyes on Jesus, our leader and instructor. He was willing to die a shameful death on the cross because of the joy he knew would be his afterwards; and now he sits in the place of honor by the throne of God.

THE HERON

The water birds called herons
(There are several kinds)
Are slender with long necks and bills,
And very short tails behind.

They are adapted for wading,
And feed on frogs and fish.
They use their bills more as a vise—
To catch whatever they wish.

They have a custom at breeding time
Of adopting a "standing ground."
All of them face one direction,
And none of them turn around.

There are many species of herons. Some have evolved as marsh-dwelling waders, and others make use of trees for nests and as perches. The different species often live in mixed groups. They measure from sixteen to fifty inches in height, depending on the species. They all have long, broad wings. Toward breeding time the adult birds gather in one vicinity. As bird after bird arrives, they stand facing in the same direction, just waiting. Then the males leave to occupy nests, or nesting sites, where the females join them. Why the strange waiting stance? No one knows exactly why, except that it is a custom always observed. We too should ever face in the same direction, keeping our eyes on Jesus, our leader and instructor. He will keep us on the right path and lead us home when the time is ripe.

Dear Heavenly Father, I love You and praise You. I pray that I may be a good student and apply the message of Your Word to the best of my ability, that my life may be a shining light for You.

PSALMS 89:1,2 Forever and ever I will sing about the tender kindness of the Lord! Young and old shall hear about your blessings. Your love and kindness are forever; your truth is as enduring as the heavens.

THE HOOPOE

An Old World bird, the hoopoe
Presents a striking pose.
He holds his handsome fan-shaped crest
Erect wherever he goes.

He was used in hieroglyphics,
By Egyptians of the day,
And is mentioned in the Bible,
In a most familiar way.

This bird is a cinnamon pink
With black- and white-striped wings.
His tail is black- and white-striped too,
And he's named for the song he sings.

The hoopoe is a beautiful bird from ten to twelve inches long. It flies in a peculiar butterflylike fashion, which makes its coloring appear even more striking. Hoopoes are named for their strange call—a soft, low "hoop-hoop-hoop." There is also a harsh warning call that sounds like a cat's meow. The hoopoe has an unusual method of defense. When threatened by a hawk or other bird of prey, the bird will sit on the ground with wings and tail spread. The head is thrown back and the bill pointed in the air. Just as the hoopoe throws back its head and directs its bill to Heaven in times of trouble, we too can direct our prayers to Heaven and find our defense in Him. So often we say, "All we can do now is pray." Prayer should be the first thing we do, not the last—and it is always the most effective thing we can do!

Dear Father, help me to remember when I am in trouble or danger that You have provided an avenue of communication and strength through prayer. Help me to always keep that avenue open and active.

EPHESIANS 6:11,13 Put on all of God's armor so that you will be able to stand safe against all strategies and tricks of Satan. . . . So use every piece of God's armor to resist the enemy whenever he attacks, and when it is all over, you will still be standing up.

THE HORNBILL

The hornbill is a bird so smart,
It's difficult to believe!
She lives in deepest Africa,
And nests in the baobab tree.

When ready to lay her eggs, she finds
A hole deep in the heart,
And using mud, seals herself in,
Her family to start.

She leaves a tiny little slit,
And her mate brings her food
While she sits and hatches out
Her little hornbill brood.

She stays with them until they grow
Enough to learn to fend;
She pecks a hole and leaves the nest—
They seal it up again.

They're safe from harm 'til they emerge
As independent birds.
Now isn't that as incredible
As anything you have heard?

The female hornbill may make as many as forty trips a day for mud with which to seal her nest. When the opening is just big enough to wiggle into, she squeezes through and finishes sealing it from the inside, leaving only a tiny slit for food. There she is safe from harm and can raise her family in peace, depending on the male for her daily food. So should we seal ourselves within the armor of God, taking full advantage of the spiritual protection He offers us and feeding daily on His Word and prayer, fully depending on Him.

Dear Heavenly Father, help me to take this example from nature and use it in my life. Give me the peace that passes all understanding, and help me to be spiritually nourished through constant communication with You in prayer and the reading of Your Word. I praise You for the blessing of Your protection.

JOB 12:10,11 For the soul of every living thing is in the hand of God, and the breath of all mankind. Just as my mouth can taste good food, so my mind tastes truth when I hear it.

THE INDRI

The natives of Madagascar
Treat the indri with dread.
They believe he carries souls
Of their ancestors who are dead.

Indri is Malagasy,
Meaning "There it is!" you see.
They say "Throw a spear at it,
And he'll return it with accuracy!"

An indri moves by leaping,
Pushing off with his hind feet.
He has a long and mournful call
That he's often known to repeat.

The indri is the largest of the lemurs, growing up to thirty inches in length plus the addition of a short tail. It has long hind legs with grasping feet. The general effect of its color is black and white, although pure white albinos have been known. The natives of Madagascar view the indri as sacred and believe that it carries the souls of their ancestors. Praise God, we know better than that! Job says (Job 12:10,11) that our souls are in the hands of God, and what better place! He gives us the peace that passes all understanding, and we need not fear for we rest on the promises in His Word. There are many sayings and folktales surrounding the indri, such as the one about the spear, but with the truth of God, we are freed from superstition and fear—and brought into the Light of Truth.

Dear Heavenly Father, thank You for Your Word, upon which we can trust and rely without fail. May we learn to ever respect Your Truth, and reject the lies of the devil. Help us to rightly divine the Word of Truth.

PROVERBS 20:7 It is a wonderful heritage to have an honest father.

THE JACANA

The jacana, or the lily-trotter,
Called lotus bird as well,
Has seven known cousin groups
As far as we can tell.

This bird has feet that are not webbed,
And toes and nails so long
That he can walk on floating leaves,
Though leaves are not that strong!

The male is faithful to the nest.
The female goes her way—
She may fill ten nests with eggs,
Stopping only to lay.

There are several species of jacanas, tropical aberrant wading birds: the American jacana, the African, the Lesser African, the pheasant-tailed, the bronze-winged, the Madagascar and the lotus-bird. They vary from six and a half to twelve inches in length, except for the pheasant-tailed, whose eight-inch tail brings it to twenty-one inches overall. Their specialized feet enable them to walk on water plants without sinking. The nests are often little islands of plants and debris floating in the water. The male hatches the eggs in most cases, while the female goes her way. The baby jacana has an honest and caring father to hatch and raise it. We have the wonderful heritage of the Heavenly Father to watch over us. He knows us from before we were conceived and through all eternity. He gives peace everlasting, and if we trust Him, we have nothing to dread or fear.

Dear Lord, thank You for the security and love that You provide to Your children. I pray that I might have faith in You as I step "from lily pad to lily pad" in this life on earth.

PSALMS 109:21 But as for me, O Lord, deal with me as your child, as one who bears your name! Because you are so kind, O Lord, deliver me.

THE JAGUARUNDI

Though jaguarundi is his name,
He's more like an otter to me.
He is an excellent swimmer,
And in forest or swamp runs free.

Some people call him "otter cat."
From the water, he seldom strays.
He's a solitary creature,
Except in mating forays.

His body is elongated,
And the head is long and low.
He averages about a yard in length—
Eleven inches from shoulder to toe.

There are two color phases,
But one litter can have both—
Some black or gray, some chestnut—
But they're alike in growth.

The jaguarundi is certainly nothing like a jaguar! How it came to be named after it is hard to understand. Its coat is not patterned and may range from black to gray or from tawny to chestnut. A single litter may contain both families of color. The jaguarundi feeds on small mammals and game birds. It is found in the extreme southwest of the United States and in South America. Indeed, the jaguarundi is nothing like the jaguar it is named for. We, however, were created in God's image. We bear the name *Christian* as followers of Christ. We should strive to follow His example in everything we do—that others may see Christ in us.

Dear Heavenly Father, I pray that You will deal with me as Your Own child, guiding and protecting me through my days. I thank You for the great honor of being called Christian and for the responsibility that comes with it, for I know that only as I obey Your Word will I grow in Your grace.

EPHESIANS 2:13 But now you belong to Christ Jesus, and though you once were far away from God, now you have been brought very near to him because of what Jesus Christ has done for you with his blood.

THE "JOEY"
(Baby Kangaroo)

The parents are called kangaroos,
Australia is called home.
A marsupial, Mama has a pouch
So "joey" cannot roam.

The tiny little newborn 'roo—
Naked, yes, and blind,
Only one inch long at birth,
Yet he the pouch must find.

He leaves the birth canal and crawls,
Alone and without aid,
Into the shelter of the fold,
Where he will be repaid.

Repaid with food and warmth and care,
"Joey" will remain
Inside the pouch for four long months
Before venturing out again.

It is amazing that this helpless little "joey"—as the baby kangaroo is called—at one inch long and about one thirty-fifth of an ounce in weight—can make its long journey into its mother's pouch. And yet we make a long journey also, from the cold world of sin into the warmth of Jesus' love. We must each do it alone—for no one else can make the trip for us. Once inside the fold of Christ, we feed first on milk and then on the meat of the Word, growing each day just as the little "joey." Even after we have ventured back out into the world, we must return every so often to the fold for renewal and protection. As the "joey" grows older, its mother eventually refuses to let it return to the pouch. Praise to our Father that He never severs us from His love and care!

Dear Lord, I thank You for the shelter of the fold. I praise You for being near when I need You and for providing me with Your Word when I am spiritually hungry. Help me to be open to Your teachings at all times.

II TIMOTHY 2:19 But God's truth stands firm like a great rock, and nothing can shake it. It is a foundation stone with these words written on it: "The Lord knows those who are really his," and "A person who calls himself a Christian should not be doing things that are wrong."

THE KLIPSPRINGER

*Klipspringers love to scale the rocks—
They live in cliff ravines.
Their hoofs are made especially
For this kind of life, it seems.*

*They're even surer-footed
Than the surest mountain goat.
They spring aloft with all four feet,
And have a mosslike coat.*

*It will come away in tufts
And soon replace itself.
It is an added protection
As they spring from shelf to shelf.*

*It serves as a soft, safe cushion
Against the rocks and thorns.
It often confuses the enemy,
And also, it adorns.*

Because the hair on this small antelope is springy and light enough for mattresses and saddles, the klipspringer was once eagerly hunted. It has species in Tanganyika, Northern Nigeria to the Sudan, Ethiopia and Somalia south to the Cape. It has adapted to life on bare and inaccessible rocky places. It springs on all four feet, and it has been said that the klipspringer can land on a pinnacle no larger than the size of a silver dollar. It is very careful and knows a steady rock when it sees one! We too should know a firm foundation when we see it—and the surest foundation of all is God's truth. When we stand on our Rock, Jesus Christ, we can be sure that we will not slip and fall. It is only when we move from our Rock that our position becomes precarious.

Dear Heavenly Father, I thank you for providing me with a firm foundation—the great Rock of Your Son, Jesus Christ, my Redeemer!

LUKE 12:25,26 And besides, what's the use of worrying? What good does it do? Will it add a single day to your life? Of course not! And if worry can't even do such little things as that, what's the use of worrying over bigger things?

THE LIMPKIN

The limpkin limps along
With a strange, uneven gait,
Gingerly treading across the swamp
As though he might be late.

Lifting long toes in the air,
He nervously twitches his tail.
He can swim, but he'd rather not.
He's linked to the crane and the rail.

Flying's not for him—
He can if he really must;
But once in a tree, he runs along
The branches with perfect trust.

They call him the crying, or wailing, bird—
"Mad widow" in Mexico.
His cry has the sound of sadness
As it rings in the moonlight glow.

The limpkin is a marsh bird. It was once common in Georgia and Florida until it was hunted for food. Now there are sanctuaries such as the Everglades National Park, where the swamps are not drained. The limpkin feeds on snails and other mollusks. It has an eerie, wailing call, usually used at night and described as having "a quality of unutterable sadness." Folklore says the cries are of little children lost in the swamp forever. No wonder they call the limpkin the "crying bird," or the "wailing bird." Some people might come under that name too. They cry inconsolably and are filled with fear and pessimism. God tells us we need not worry but to trust in Him. His Word is so clear if we will but heed it!

Dear Lord, help me to put the future in Your hands and live today for You, without worry for tomorrow. Should I start to cry or wail in fear over the future, remind me, Lord, that the future is in Your hands, and so am I!

II SAMUEL 22:2,3 Jehovah is my rock, my fortress and my Savior. I will hide in God, who is my rock and my refuge. He is my shield and my salvation, my refuge and high tower. Thank you, O my Savior, for saving me from all my enemies.

THE LING

The ling belongs to the cod family,
And he's up to seven feet long.
As a fish, he was a noble dish
And often served with song.

Henry the Eighth preferred him
To serve to his honored guests.
Ling was considered a delicacy,
And was usually devoured with zest.

The ling is strange in his habits.
He likes his back to the wall.
He needs it to be—for security.
He's not too brave at all!

Today the ling is described as "commercially valuable." During the reign of Henry the Eighth, however, things were different. Salted ling was considered a delicacy in the royal courts and held in high esteem. This creature is found in the northeast Atlantic. It lives at depths from three hundred to six hundred feet. The ling will invariably seek out a place where its body will come in contact with a hard object. This is called the "rodent" habit. It seems to need the security of a rock, a sunken ship, or some other object at its back. It needs a "backup." We have the greatest "backup" of all! God is always with us, if we just ask. He offers us security in this insecure world.

Dear Heavenly Father, like the ling, I need a solid rock to hold to, and I thank You for providing it. I know that with Your support I can handle anything that comes my way. I pray that I may continue to grow and that I may help others to grow by sharing with them my faith in You.

PSALMS 18:33 He gives me the surefootedness of a mountain goat upon the crags. He leads me safely along the top of the cliffs.

THE MOUNTAIN GOAT

The mountain goat is sure of foot,
A steeplejack supreme.
He scales the dizzy mountain heights
Though impossible it may seem.

He really looks quite clumsy,
But of high peaks, he's the king.
He rarely makes a misstep—
He doesn't miss a thing.

His concave toes are suction cups
And cling at the steepest height.
This fleecy, shaggy creature
Is a mountaineer's delight!

The mountain goat is North America's surest-footed climber. It can scale amazing heights while scarcely disturbing a pebble. It "looks before it leaps" and rarely makes a mistake in its travels. It has confidence in its judgment and does not falter. So may we have confidence in the Holy Spirit. Because He lives in us, we can have trust in ourselves. Indecision is an enemy for we have His Word to show us the Way.

Dear Lord, help me to have the confidence and sure-footedness of the mountain goat. Help me to follow Your leading in my life with no hesitation—but help me to also "look before I leap" and use the common sense You provided me with.

I JOHN 4:18,19 We need have no fear of someone who loves us perfectly; his perfect love for us eliminates all dread of what he might do to us. If we are afraid, it is for fear of what he might do to us, and shows that we are not fully convinced that he really loves us. So you see, our love for him comes as a result of his loving us first.

THE NATTERJACK TOAD

The natterjack has short hind legs,
And does not jump, but runs.
He can be extremely fast
But is lazy when he suns.

This toad seems to migrate
And move from place to place.
Without a scientific reason,
He changes his home base.

He is found in Europe,
And he's just three inches long.
When alarmed, he fills with air;
When handled, his odor is strong.

Down his back is a yellow line,
His trademark, so to speak.
Have you ever known someone
Who had a "yellow streak"?

The natterjack is sometimes known as the running toad. Because its short hind legs are not conducive to jumping, it runs down its prey—spiders, insects, worms, and snails. The natterjack is confined to Europe. It is easily recognizable because of the yellow streak down the back. Many people equate a yellow streak to cowardice or fear. We need not fear God, for He has shown His great love for us by the gift of His Son. We must not confuse fear with awe, though. We do indeed stand in awe of God, for He is a righteous judge and will judge us for our deeds and thoughts. Because He loves us, He will judge us fairly and impartially. Let us hold Him in great respect—with love, not fear, in our hearts.

Dear Heavenly Father, I pray that I may be strong in the faith and give You all my love and respect. I pray that I may show no "yellow streak" but always witness bravely for You and Your Word.

PSALMS 7:10 God is my shield; he will defend me. He saves those whose hearts and lives are true and right.

THE NORTH AMERICAN PIKA

The North American pika
Lives on the mountain slope.
Hiding in the rock debris,
He has learned to cope.

He's a small animal,
A cousin to the hare.
The pika's ears are short and round—
His tail just isn't there!

He's found in western America
Above seven thousand feet.
He's safe from harm in his rocky abode.
It's a warm and safe retreat.

Haying in the meadow,
He carries grass to his home
To store away for a snowy day,
When it's unsafe to roam.

The North American pika is an interesting little animal. It emits several different cries and seems to have a language all its own. Although it has many predators, the only really dangerous one is the weasel, as it can follow the pika down through the rocks. Still, the pika is small enough and fast enough to elude this enemy in most cases. The pika never emits a distress call when chased by a weasel. Any other predator, however, will set off in the pika a series of warning cries. The rocks shield the little creature from its enemies just as God shields us. He is our defense in times of trouble and strife. We call and He is there. He hears the language of our hearts.

Dear Lord, I thank You and praise You for providing me with a hiding place when I am fearful—for understanding my heart's cries and answering in love. I know those answers are always good for me, even though they may not be what I want to hear at the time.

DEUTERONOMY 31:8 Don't be afraid, for the Lord will go before you and will be with you; he will not fail nor forsake you.

THE OPOSSUM

See the hairy 'possum
Hanging on a limb?
He'll soon go searching for his food,
And predators watch for him.

He has many enemies,
But he has a defense.
He falls into a hypnotic state—
Terror makes him tense.

He might play dead for hours
Until the danger's past.
Then he'll unroll and wobble home,
Safe again at last!

The 'possum is a regular slowpoke. Its legs are so short that its belly almost touches the ground as it ambles along. At the sight of danger, the funny little creature rolls into a ball, playing dead. Scientists now think that it is sheer terror that causes this phenomenon. The 'possum is virtually paralyzed with fear. We, on the other hand, do not have to be afraid for we have God's promise that we will never be alone. What a tremendous promise this is! No matter how great our foe or how big our troubles, God will be with us. Praise the Lord!

Dear Heavenly Father, I thank You for Your everlasting love and protection. Help me to stand boldly in the face of adversity, knowing that You are standing beside me. I pray that I might be a strong and productive Christian, trusting You always.

REVELATION 2:10b Remain faithful even when facing death and I will give you the crown of life—an unending, glorious future.

THE OSPREY

This remarkable bird of prey
Lives almost completely on fish.
Known as a fish hawk in America,
That is his favorite dish.

He hunts, circling over the water,
Keeping an eye out for prey.
Then, finding it, he plunges
To triumphantly bear it away.

Some ospreys live in colonies,
With nests built of seaweed and sticks.
The parents feed them the first eight weeks,
And then it's up to the chicks.

When the osprey learns to fly at seven or eight weeks, it either finds its own fish or dies. The parents are through with it. Their job is finished. In flight, the adult has a wing span of about five feet, the size of a small eagle. The osprey was becoming scarce, but with a little help from man, it is building up its numbers again. This bird is a highly effective hunter; ninety percent of its dives are successful. It is dedicated to the task of survival, and quite a task it is. Fish have been found with osprey remains on their backs, the talons dug in too deep to let go and the fish too big to conquer. The ospreys were submerged and drowned. Oh, that we could hold on to the Christian life in that way! No matter what happens, even death itself, we can cling to our Christian principles and ideals and not let loose. What a glorious prize is waiting for the faithful!

Dear Heavenly Father, help me to cleave to You with the tenacity of the osprey, that I may attain the crown of life You have offered us.

II SAMUEL 22:47 The Lord lives. Blessed be my Rock. Praise to him—the Rock of my salvation.

THE OSTRICH

The ostrich is a marvelous bird,
And he loves to dance.
He dances for no reason at all.
For love, he'll really prance!

He dances with his lady love
To let her know he cares.
It's she who starts the mating game,
But he instinctively shares.

When the ostrich wants to hide,
He bends down to the ground.
He looks like a rock from the distance,
And usually won't be found.

The picture we sometimes see of an ostrich standing with its head in the sand is untrue. It will crouch with its neck tight to the ground, thus becoming unobtrusive and blending in with the surroundings. From a short distance it looks like a rock. We praise the Lord that we have the true Rock, Jesus Christ. He is the same yesterday, today, and forever, and we can put our full trust in Him. He does not just look like a rock—He *is* a Rock!

Dear Lord, thank You so much for being my Rock—unshakable and unchanging in this shaky, changeable world. Help me to hold tight to You wherever I go—in whatever I do. What a joy to know that You are always with me and that You care about what happens to me. I can face anything, Lord, with You as my Rock and my fortress.

AMOS 4:13 For you are dealing with the one who formed the mountains and made the winds, and knows your every thought; he turns the morning to darkness and crushes down the mountains underneath his feet: Jehovah, the Lord, the God of Hosts, is his name.

THE PELICAN

The pelican may seem clumsy,
But in flight he is superb.
In the water, he's a marvel—
A really miraculous bird!

His bill expands into a pouch,
A dip net to catch food.
The bill can hold eight quarts of fish
For the pelican and his brood.

This bird is one of the biggest—
Up to six feet long!
His wing span may be ten feet wide,
And the pelican is strong!

His nest is large and cumbersome,
On the ground or in low trees.
Pelicans are very sociable,
And live in large colonies.

The pelican, large as it is, is a superb flyer although its food is obtained from the water. It uses thermal air currents to soar upward in spirals as high as eight thousand feet, where it may circle for hours, flapping and gliding. It rides high on the wind. And it is the God who made that wind Who loves us—Who sent His Son to die for us. What great and precious miracle is this, that the Creator of the universe should love us so much? Praise God for this miracle!

Dear Heavenly Father, when I try to think out my life and handle things by myself, like the pelican, I fly in circles. Help me to turn it all over to You and to realize that I do not have to understand why You love me—I just need to know that You do!

JAMES 1:5-8 If you want to know what God wants you to do, ask him, and he will gladly tell you, for he is always ready to give a bountiful supply of wisdom to all who ask him; he will not resent it. But when you ask him, be sure that you really expect him to tell you, for a doubtful mind will be as unsettled as a wave of the sea that is driven and tossed by the wind; and every decision you then make will be uncertain, as you turn first this way, and then that. If you don't ask with faith, don't expect the Lord to give you any solid answer.

THE PHALAROPE

The roles of the sexes are reversed
In the phalarope family.
The female is more colorful
And behaves more aggressively.

These pretty birds are waders,
Though they prefer to swim.
They float high on the water,
And are often seen to spin.

They create a small whirlpool
To bring their food in view.
They float upon the ocean waves
The entire winter through.

The phalarope is a small wader with a needle-shaped bill. There are three species, ranging from six and a half to ten inches long. In the winter they are quite dull in hue, but the summer brings a beautiful and colorful coat. Although they are classed as waders, they do not actually wade, but swim. They have a habit of spinning around in the water like a top when, it is surmised, they may be snapping up insects or stirring up food from the bottom. They float very high in the water because of their dense plumage, and often they are swept far across the Atlantic Ocean by winds and gales, tossed to and fro. We too can be tossed to and fro by the winds of indecision if we fail to place our faith in God. Faith is the compass that steers us through the rocks and shoals to Christ. We must have faith in God if we are to claim His promises!

Dear Heavenly Father, I pray for the faith to step out and do Your will, knowing full well that I am not alone. I will not be tossed by uncertainty and doubt but will maintain a steady course toward that Star of Bethlehem.

II CORINTHIANS 12:10b For when I am weak, then I am strong—the less I have, the more I depend on him [Christ].

THE PILOT FISH

Does the pilot fish guide a whale or shark,
Or just go along for the ride?
This black- and white-striped creature
Is always found by their side.

He'll stick with a ship or a manta ray—
Anything big in size.
Is he really piloting?
I wonder where the truth lies.

Over any object's surface
A boundary layer moves
At the same speed as the object—
I wonder what this proves?

Has the pilot fish found the secret
Of efficient travel per se?
He gets a long distance faster
Than he could any other way.

The pilot fish is still a mystery. It is known only that it always swims close to a large object, animate or inanimate. It may be for speed, as it stays within the boundary layer, or for protection. Whatever the reason, there you will find the pilot fish. We too must stay close, but our companion is Christ. We follow in His shadow, knowing that He provides us not only with our daily needs, but with life itself!

Dear Heavenly Father, thank You for bringing me close in Your love and protection. Fill me with Your Spirit that I might share it with others as we move on our journey toward You.

LUKE 6:39b What good is it for one blind man to lead another? He will fall into a ditch and pull the other down with him.

THE PILOT WHALE

A sociable creature, the pilot whale—
A dolphin when the truth is told.
He has an age-old habit
Of following with the fold.

If a panicky brother leads him to shore,
He will follow along like a sheep.
It often becomes a mass suicide
For this denizen of the deep.

If man tries to rescue him,
And pull him to safety once more,
He paddles right back to the others,
And again beaches himself on the shore.

The pilot whale is also called the blackfish and may grow to twenty-eight feet in length. It has a bulging forehead that forms a dome overhanging the mouth. This large creature of the sea is a follower, and it is seen in many parts of the world. It has been reported that a male acts as the leader, but it has been found that a pilot whale will follow any member of the group that happens to lead it. Doesn't that sound like the human animal? Most of us are also easily led. We must be careful of those we follow, though—and of those to whom we listen—or we are likely to be in trouble. Only when we follow our Lord's Word can we be certain that we are headed in the right direction.

Dear Lord, I pray that I may ever continue in Your counsel. Help me to keep my eyes and ears open . . . to stay alert for false teachings . . . to use the Spirit's wisdom in studying the Word. I pray that I may be a follower only of You, Lord.

PROVERBS 29:25 Fear of man is a dangerous trap, but to trust in God means safety.

THE PORCUPINE

Porky's reputation
Is really quite a shame.
People may get frightened
At the mere sound of his name.

And yet he's really friendly
Unless he grows alarmed.
His spiny coat lies smoothly
When he feels he won't be harmed.

The porcupine has armor—
Thirty thousand quills—
That stand up at his bidding
And give his enemies the chills!

He's usually quite unruffled
And makes a friendly pet,
But do not irritate him,
Or you'll wish you'd never met!

The porcupine is equipped with a unique security system. In the presence of an adversary, it simply turns its back, lifts its fearsome quills—and is safe from attack! We also are equipped with a "security system." We are equipped with God's Holy Word, and when Satan attacks, all we have to do is call upon the power of God, just as the porcupine calls upon its deadly barbs. We must trust in the Lord and be ready to use His Word as a protection against sin and temptation whenever they appear.

Dear Lord, please help me to be friendly and to show Your love to all I meet, but help me, Lord, to also realize that Satan is real and that he is a fearsome adversary. Help me to study Your Word and have it foremost in my heart and mind when I need to use my "security system" as the porcupine does.

PSALMS 13:5 But I will always trust in you and in your mercy and shall rejoice in your salvation.

THE RHINOCEROS

*The rhino is a vanishing breed—
An odd-looking animal, indeed!*

*He has great folds of hairless skin,
And he is anything but thin!*

*He is short-sighted, but survives well
Because of his hearing and sense of smell.*

*His great horn has a mighty thrust—
His temperament, you just can't trust!*

*He changes character quite fast—
Good humor never seems to last!*

The rhinoceros is the second largest land animal in the world. It is totally unpredictable. It may be friendly and docile one minute and charge ferociously the next. It is amazingly agile for its size and not too bright. It is definitely not to be trusted!

Dear Lord, Creator of all, I love and praise You for being so trustworthy. For always being my friend and my Savior. For the grace You show toward me, no matter how I may irritate You with my immature actions. Thank You for Your forgiveness and love. As the rhino is the epitomy of ugliness and untrustworthiness, so You are the epitomy of beauty and truth!

PSALMS 25:4,5 Show me the path where I should go, O Lord; point out the right road for me to walk. Lead me; teach me; for you are the God who gives me salvation. I have no hope except in you.

THE ROADRUNNER

A member of the species
Called the cuckoo birds,
The roadrunner eats lizards,
And rattlesnakes too, I've heard.

You may see this creature
In country hot and dry.
He is usually on the ground
For he can barely fly.

He hurries on his way—
His stilted legs are strong,
And when he's really running,
You'll lose him before long!

It is so easy to be swayed by the pressures of our busy world. Like the roadrunner, we find ourselves running here and there, always in high gear. We sometimes forget why or where we are going—we just go. With God as our guide and teacher, however, we have purpose and direction in our lives. He may not always make the path smooth and easy, but He will give us the strength and courage to follow where He leads—through sorrow and joy. We can travel with a clear conscience and our heads held high when we are on His road for we know where we are going, and why!

Dear Heavenly Father, I honor You for your steadfast love and care. I pray that You will keep me on Your road and help me to be a good witness to You, that others may join me on the journey to Heaven.

PSALMS 119:1–3 Happy are all who perfectly follow the laws of God. Happy are all who search for God, and always do his will, rejecting compromise with evil, and walking only in his paths.

THE ROBIN

We talk about the robin
As the harbinger of spring;
Nothing sounds so very sweet
As the song we hear him sing.

He sings that winter's over
And that sunny days will come.
He's usually among the very first
To return when winter's done.

He is always welcome,
With his rosy vest so bright,
As he sings with sweet abandon
To the sparkling of the light.

Yes, each year the pretty little robin flies south for the winter, and each year we watch impatiently for its return in the springtime. It seems to have a built-in timer that tells it just when to appear. The robin follows the laws of nature that God has laid out for it. No wonder it sings! We too can sing with happy hearts and clear consciences when we are following the Lord. What a joy to go to Him in prayer and share our lives with Him! As the robin returns with each springtime, so God renews and refreshes our spirits with His love when we turn to Him in hope and trust.

Dear Lord, help me to remember Your promises and to draw upon them. Thank you for restoring my courage when I need it the most. And I thank You with all my heart for being my trusted companion and champion on this road of life.

II CORINTHIANS 4:8,9 We are pressed on every side by troubles, but not crushed and broken. We are perplexed because we don't know why things happen as they do, but we don't give up and quit. We are hunted down, but God never abandons us. We get knocked down, but we get up again and keep going.

THE STARFISH

The starfish is a creature
Of beauty and of awe.
His structure is so different,
He defies every law.

His shape is quite unique—
A perfect star display—
And yet he walks and eats,
And mollusks are his prey.

He creeps on the floor of the ocean
With suction-tipped delight;
He can't see where he's going,
But can tell day from night.

The starfish is an enigma. When it is injured, torn, or broken, it simply renews itself. It can be torn in two and each half will slowly regenerate—until it again becomes whole. As Christians, we also have the ability to withstand trials and tribulations and to "regenerate"—drawing on the Holy Spirit for strength and healing. The problems of the world cannot defeat us spiritually as the Holy Spirit abides within our hearts to renew us . . . to stimulate new growth . . . to once more make us whole in Jesus Christ.

Dear Lord, I thank You for the many times You have lifted me up and set me on my feet again . . . for the many times you have "kissed the hurt" and made it well . . . for taking my shattered life and putting the pieces together once more. As the starfish reflects the beautiful Star of Bethlehem, help me to reflect the wondrous love and compassion of the Savior.

PSALMS 32:8 I will instruct you (says the Lord) and guide you along the best pathway for your life; I will advise you and watch your progress.

THE STILT

If you ever see a stilt,
Your impulse will be laughter.
With his long and skinny legs,
You'll wonder what he's after.

And yet his gait is graceful,
As he wades up to his "knees,"
And in the air, those long legs
Make maneuvering a breeze.

He uses them as a rudder,
For steering and to guide—
God knew what He was doing,
When the stilt He diversified!

The stilt is a wader with long, long legs and a long, straight bill. All species are primarily black and white. They are found in Africa, southern Europe and Asia, and from the southern United States to northern South America, including the Galapagos and the West Indies, as well as in New Zealand and Australia. They live in pairs or in small flocks around shallow waters, feeding on water insects and small crustaceans. They also eat caterpillars from the surrounding bushes and plants. The long legs of the stilt have a twofold purpose. They help it to wade deeper into the water, hence aid in feeding, and they are used as a rudder in flight, as a guide in steering and maneuvering the stilt while it is in the air. We also have a rudder—Jesus Christ. He promises to keep us on course and to help us along the way if we will just open our hearts to Him. The Holy Spirit is with us constantly to aid us in making our decisions. Let us use our "rudder" in all that we do and not let it lay idle.

Dear Heavenly Father, I thank You for seeing the needs of Your creatures and for filling those needs. As the stilt makes use of its "rudder," help me to make use of my Guide!

JEREMIAH 8:7a The stork knows the time of her migration, as does the turtledove, and the crane, and the swallow. They all return at God's appointed time each year.

THE STORK

Long regarded as a symbol
Of good luck and fertility,
The stork has been encouraged
To raise her family.

They nest upon the housetops
In Europe's countryside.
The residents provide platforms
On which they can abide.

The birds migrate each winter
To a more conducive clime,
But seem to know when to return,
And where, time after time.

There are several species of stork, the best known being the white stork of legend. It has long been regarded as a symbol of fertility and good luck. In Europe, where a stork census was taken for many years, people used to anchor huge baskets to their roofs for the storks to nest in. The migration of the white stork is well known because the bird is easily seen and many of them have been ringed. Storks make their way to Africa, traveling across the Bosphorus and the Straits of Gibralter to avoid long sea journeys. A few stay there to breed, but most of them return to their homes in Europe when the time comes. Many return to the same areas—even to the same nests. They follow God's leading, and it never fails them. We too should follow His leading in our lives. We need no symbols of good luck for we have the reality of the Holy Spirit. We know that "luck" is fickle—but God is not!

Dear Lord, what a relief it is to simply put my trust in You and follow Your leading! I need no symbol of good luck. My trustworthy Bible—Your Word—is my guide!

DEUTERONOMY 33:27a The eternal God is your Refuge, and underneath are the everlasting arms.

THE TAILORBIRD

Those funny little tailorbirds
Sing a monotonous song.
There are nine species known,
And their tails are all quite long.

They have a special talent
That really is unique—
They use green leaves to make a nest,
Fastening them with their beak.

They sew the leaves to make a pouch,
Using fiber or spider web.
They make a "stitch," each half an inch,
To make their eggs a bed.

And so the nest hangs on the branch
With a leafy canopy.
A "living nest" of sweet green leaves—
Refuge for their family!

The tailorbird is an inconspicuous little warbler about five and a half inches long, with a long bill and a long tail. Its song is a shrill "cheewit" that is repeated over and over. The remarkable feature of this little bird is its nest-building ability. It fastens living leaves together with rivetlike stitches to provide a nest and canopy. It may use one large leaf or as many as forty-five small ones to build its little living refuge. Indeed, we too have a Living Refuge in God, our Father. What a wonderful concept! For truly He provides a "living nest"—a place of safety—and underneath are spread His everlasting arms!

Dear Lord, what a beautiful thing You have done in providing us with a Living Refuge, our place of solace and safety. I will ever draw my strength and courage from Your lovingkindness.

MATTHEW 6:34 So don't be anxious about tomorrow. God will take care of your tomorrow too. Live one day at a time.

THE WOODCHUCK

The woodchuck has another name—
The groundhog is the very same.

He hibernates the winter through—
Four to six months is often true.

He sleeps so deep, he can't feel or hear.
He hardly breathes 'til spring is near.

But don't depend on Groundhog Day—
He can't forecast as people say.

He may come out to eat, you see,
And then decide he's still sleepy!

Why are we so anxious to know the future? Just as some hopeful but foolish people depend on Groundhog Day to forecast the weather, others listen to fortune tellers and false prophets and take them seriously. But only God knows what tomorrow will bring, and we have no need to be anxious or concerned about it. If we live today to the best of our ability, tomorrow will be taken care of. Look at how He cares for the woodchuck!

Dear Father in Heaven, I thank You so much for the assurance of Your love and care. Sometimes I forget, Lord, to "let go and let God," and then I try to mold my future instead of putting it in Your hands. I know that You expect me to do my very best, with the help of the Holy Spirit. I pray that I may not disappoint You.

2
Love

ACTS 4:32 All the believers were of one heart and mind, and no one felt that what he owned was his own; everyone was sharing.

THE APOSTLEBIRD

The Australian apostlebirds
Build a nest of mud and grass.
They live together in harmonious groups
And do not have a social caste.

They are known by another name
For the way they keep together—
They're called "happy families."
They are truly "birds of a feather."

They build their structure upon a limb,
And they communally start to nest.
They are not the greatest fliers,
But at living, they're the best!

The name "apostlebird" apparently comes from the fact that these birds usually travel in flocks of twelve. Fluffy and gray, they live in harmonious groups and are highly sociable. They feed on insects and seeds. They are clumsy runners and weak fliers. The group nests communally in a basin-shaped mud and grass structure. When resting, they huddle together and preen one another. They are truly "happy families." We as Christians like to be known as "happy families" too—caring and sharing with one another not because we have to but because we want to! The rewards of sharing are priceless. It is true that the more love we give, the more love we receive. Try it and see for yourself!

Dear Lord, help me to be unselfish with all that I have. I pray that I may learn to think of others first—before I think of self. Help me to learn to share with an open heart and an open hand. What a wonderful example You have given us in the apostlebird! Thank You.

PROVERBS 17:17 A true friend is always loyal, and a brother is born to help in time of need.

THE BLUE WHALE

The largest mammal known today
Is the great blue whale.
He may measure one hundred feet
From his head to his swishing tail.

This giant of the ocean depths
Is faithful to the end.
If another whale is wounded,
He'll stay with his wounded friend.

Whalers have found in their journeys at sea
That when they spear a blue,
Another one will linger near,
Until the blue whale's life is through.

Thank goodness that the practice of whaling has been curbed, for these great creatures of the sea were becoming scarce. Many whalers in early days found that if they harpooned a whale, it was easy to kill a second one for it would stay with its wounded mate or companion until death. These huge mammals are gentle, and they seem to be caring creatures, always loyal to one another. The largest blue whale ever measured was some one hundred feet in length, and the largest ever weighed totaled over a hundred and thirty-six tons! (It had to be weighed in sections.) The newborn is usually around twenty-five feet in length and lives exclusively on milk for almost six months. Truly an amazing mammal!

Dear Heavenly Father, I thank You that I have true friends, and I pray that I might be as true to them as they are to me. Help me to keep my eyes open and realize when a brother or sister may be in need. I pray that I might not become so caught up in my own life that I overlook those around me.

PROVERBS 22:6 Teach a child to choose the right path, and when he is older he will remain upon it.

THE ELEPHANT

Behold the mighty elephant
With tusks of gleaming white.
A giant of an animal,
He's really quite a sight.

The female may weigh several tons,
Her calf, two hundred pounds.
She treats her child affectionately,
Between them, love abounds.

She watches him so carefully,
And helps him day by day.
She believes in discipline,
And he learns to obey.

They learn to be protective,
And when the old grow weak,
The younger bulls protect them—
They have a gentle streak.

The elephant has a strong protective instinct. Young bulls have been known to stay with an elder—protecting and guarding it—until it dies. Just as the mother loves and protects her young, showing compassion, so the young grow up with this compassion toward others. What a wonderful lesson this is for us! As we teach our children by word and action, instilling Christian morals and values, we know they will never forget this teaching. When they become adults, they have the choice of following or not following, but their memory cannot dispel the knowledge that has been instilled. Just as the elephant remembers what is taught, so we never forget our early training. We may choose to ignore it, but it is there in the filing boxes of our minds.

Dear Lord, help us to instill sound Christian principles in our children, that they may make use of them in their adult lives. Help us to prepare them—not just by word, Lord, but by the examples we set.

ISAIAH 11:3,4a His delight will be obedience to the Lord. He will not judge by appearance, false evidence, or hearsay, but will defend the poor and the exploited.

THE GIRAFFE

There's something about
The strange giraffe
That makes me want
To turn and laugh!

The long, long neck—
The very size—
The coloring—
The big, dark eyes!

His skin is tough
And very thick.
His greatest weapon
Is a kick.

This strange creature
Is gentle and proud.
With speed and grace
He is endowed.

If we can forget its strangeness, the giraffe is really very beautiful. Its big, soulful eyes and exceptionally long lashes would melt any heart! It is a sociable creature and lives in family groups of from four to twenty. Herds may be composed of much larger numbers. In the Book of Isaiah, David was a fair judge, not judging by appearance but by actions. Can we say as much for ourselves? Do we judge people because they are "different"? Because they are strange to us, because they look different or they have a different way of thinking? Praise the Lord for individuality! If we were all the same, it would be a very boring world! The strange-appearing character down the street may be beautiful inside—get to know him or her. Don't judge others by appearance. Think of your friends. Is it only the face they present to the word that you see, or is it the inner person—clear into the heart, where the Spirit lives?

Dear Heavenly Father, help me to be like David, a true and fair judge of others. Teach me to look beyond outside appearances and into the hearts of my neighbors. On the outside, the giraffe is a laughable creature—on the inside, sweet and gentle. Help me to remember this lesson, Lord, in all my dealings with others.

ACTS 20:35 And I was a constant example to you in helping the poor; for I remembered the words of the Lord Jesus, "It is more blessed to give than to receive."

THE HONEY ANT

In the nest of the honey ant
Some workers will not leave.
Their behavior, though peculiar,
Grants them no reprieve.

They accept the honeydew
From the hunters coming back,
Until they are distended—
A living honey sac.

They live their lives as honey pots,
That others might be fed.
When this strange pot is empty,
The honey ant is dead.

The honey ant is also called the honey-pot ant. Some of the workers, although anatomically no different from the rest, act as living storage vessels. They are called "repletes." The honey is a sugary solution obtained by the ants from aphids. When the hunters can no longer gather food, they feed from the "repletes," who truly give us an example of total unselfishness. We ourselves are not required to give to such a great extent. But we find that—in a subtler way—the more we give, the more we receive, not materially but mentally and spiritually. Any time we give spontaneously, we have a warm, contented feeling within. We feel good about ourselves and toward others. God gave us the ultimate example when He gave His Son for us, that we might have salvation.

Dear Father in Heaven, I love You and praise You for all You have given to me and—most of all—for Jesus Christ, Your Son and my Savior! Help me to give to others without thought of reimbursement but with spontaneity and joy.

PROVERBS 16:24 Kind words are like honey—enjoyable and healthful.

THE HONEYBEE

Approach the bee with caution,
He can be a fearsome thing—
Not because of the work he does,
But because of his painful sting.

The beehive is the place
To build a luscious honeycomb,
And though we look on it as food,
Bees look on it as home.

The bees are industrious—
As the drones mate with the queen,
The workers gather pollen in.
Together they make a team.

They fill the comb with honey
That is both syrupy and sweet.
Man has learned to harvest it—
It's really quite a treat!

Have you ever eaten from a honeycomb? The honey is so delicious, and it's wholesome too. And just as that honey sweetens our palates, so kind words can sweeten our hearts. We have access to a whole honeycomb of kind words, so let's use them that others may gather the benefits. Just as honey is good for the system, so kind words are good for the soul.

Dear Lord, may I think often of the bees and the honey they produce. And when I do, help me to remember that I too can produce sweetness by what I say. Teach me to use kindness in all my thoughts and actions. And please, Lord, help me to do it sincerely. Good honey must be pure, and so it is with kind words—they must be honest and true.

JOHN 13:34,35 And so I am giving a new commandment to you now—love each other just as much as I love you. Your strong love for each other will prove to the world that you are my disciples.

THE LEOPARD

"You can tell a leopard by his spots"
Is an adage old but true.
"You can tell a Christian by his life"
Is the thought I share with you.

The leopard is intelligent
And uses all his wiles;
When he's hunting for his dinner,
He uses many styles.

He may climb a tree and leap,
Or hide deep in the grass;
He'll use his spots as camouflage
Until a deer may pass.

Yes, the leopard is quite smart,
But everywhere he goes,
We all know he is a leopard—
His spots tell us so!

Just as the leopard is known by its spots, so a Christian should be known by his love. We are commanded to love one another with a spiritual love that can be seen by the world. Love is not passive—as the leopard's spots are. Love is active! *Saying* "I love you" and *showing* it are two different things.

Dear Lord, I pray that I might carry the banner of Christianity high for all to see. I want my whole life to reflect Christ, just as those beautiful spots identify the princely leopard. Help me to show my love in action as well as in words.

I CORINTHIANS 13:7 If you love someone you will be loyal to him no matter what the cost. You will always believe in him, always expect the best of him, and always stand your ground in defending him.

THE LOVEBIRD

Have you seen a parakeet
Hanging upside down,
And wondered what his problem was?
Why his head was to the ground?

He's called the hanging parakeet—
The red-faced lovebird, too.
Maybe his circulation
Gives his face that rosy hue!

There are six known species
That carry the lovebird name.
They are very friendly,
And show affection without shame.

They mate for life and spend their time
Huddled together, bill to bill.
Many are captured for taming as pets,
But the wild are numerous still.

The red-faced lovebird is the only species to roost upside down, although the Madagascar lovebird bathes by hanging upside down in the rain with its wings and tail outspread. The lovebird is about four inches long, parrotlike in form, and usually green in plumage. It acquired its name by its actions. It mates for life, and nothing can alter the couple's show of affection toward each other. We, on the other hand, are often fickle, letting circumstances get in the way of our love for each other. The Love Chapter (I Corinthians 13) tells us what true love really is. Love includes loyalty, and sometimes friends are lost because of doubt. We must learn to listen to our hearts—to ignore the voices of jealousy and malice—and be true to the love of friends and family. When we hear something derogatory about someone else, we must not jump to conclusions but, with love and kindliness, seek the truth for ourselves.

Dear Heavenly Father, teach me to be a trusted, loving friend and confidant. Help me to send forth my love into this old world of trouble and strife. I pray that I may share Your love—even in a small way—with all whose path crosses mine.

ECCLESIASTES 5:19b,20 To enjoy your work and to accept your lot in life—that is indeed a gift from God. The person who does that will not need to look back with sorrow on his past, for God gives him joy.

THE MARTIN

*The martins' path is twisting—
An aerobatic delight
Whenever they feed together
In fast and darting flight.*

*They feed on flying insects,
And catch them in the air.
They migrate where their food is,
And instinct tells them where.*

*Martins nest in colonies—
In groups they come and go
Like one big happy family,
As they dart to and fro.*

The martin seems to be full of life and energy as it darts to and fro for its supper. This small bird is a member of the swallow family, and there are several species of martins. They follow the sun and form well-developed communities, helping one another in building nests and teaching the young to fly. It seems that they are content being who they are and what they are. We too are enjoined to be content in whatever position we may be in at the moment. Sometimes that is hard to do! Our possessions and surroundings are not of great importance—but our attitudes surely are. Let us be happy with what God has given us, and joyful in Him.

Dear Heavenly Father, I thank You for all You have provided for me. Help me to be happy and content with what I have and who I am, but I pray too, Lord, that I may continue to grow in Spirit and in truth, and not become so self-satisfied that I stagnate.

HEBREWS 10:24 In response to all he has done for us, let us outdo each other in being helpful and kind to each other and in doing good.

THE OXPECKER

A faithful friend
And helper at will,
the oxpecker bird
With his bright-colored bill.

He'll perch on a host,
And it's no surprise,
That he'll rid it of pests
Like ticks and flies.

It benefits him
Throughout the day,
And helps his friend
In a welcome way.

Several oxpeckers may choose to share a host—a hippo, a zebra, or a Cape buffalo—any large animal will do. Their claws are such that they can cling anywhere in any circumstances, even upside down. They clean the host of any pests, and they also clean any wounds; as a result, the host heals more readily. The bird itself is about nine inches long, with a short, flattened bill and a long tail. The feathers are brown, but the bill is bright. There are two species, each confined to Africa: the red-billed oxpecker, which is just that; and the yellow-billed oxpecker, which has a yellow bill with a red tip. The oxpecker and its host really outdo each other in the good that comes about. Let us too give to others in any way that we can. Sharing is truly an outgrowth of Christianity. We grow as we give. As selfishness fades away, generosity and love take root, and the more we give, the more we receive in every aspect of our lives.

Dear Lord, help me to be a good and faithful friend, giving to others—as You give to me—the important things that are so easily forgotten or overlooked: encouragement, support, a pat on the back. I love You, Lord, and praise Your name.

PROVERBS 18:24 There are "friends" who pretend to be friends, but there is a friend who sticks closer than a brother.

THE PORPOISE

The porpoise is a beauty
And really seems quite tame.
A real phenomenon of grace,
He also has a brain.

He loves to gain attention,
He's really quite a ham,
Whether in the ocean depths
Or in an aquarium.

The porpoise travel in groups,
They leap and dive with glee.
They can be dangerous when aroused,
As any foe will see.

These gentle ocean creatures
Are protective of each other.
They unite against the enemy,
And fight to save a brother.

Yes, the porpoise, although large—nine to twelve feet long—is a gentle mammal, often traveling in groups of several hundred at a time. It is a united unit, and its members will help each other. When in trouble, they will surround an enemy and collectively attack by ramming. The mother is especially protective of her young and will shield it with her own body. That takes real love—to put your life in jeopardy for someone else. That is what Christ did—but He went even further. He gave His life for us that we might have eternal life in Heaven with Him. Halleluia, what a Savior!

Dear Heavenly Father, these gentle creatures have discovered how important it is to hold a united front. Help Your human children to see this truth too. We, as Christians, must take special care to hold that united front for You . . . to be in the world but not of it . . . to recognize that we need each other. As Your church, we are one, united in Christ Jesus.

PROVERBS 26:27 The man who sets a trap for others will get caught in it himself. Roll a boulder down on someone, and it will roll back and crush you.

THE PRAYING MANTIS

"Mantis" means soothsayer,
Or "prophet" in the Greek.
It refers to his attitude—
His "praying-posture" streak.

He really isn't praying,
Unless you spell it with an "e."
He's waiting for his dinner,
Whatever it may be.

With a quick snap of his forelegs
Held in that prayerful pose,
He can grasp his victim
And devour him—head to toes!

The "praying mantis" is just the opposite of what it seems to be. In its typical pose, it seems to be praying, but that is all it is—a pose. It is quietly setting a trap for its victim. Sometimes we too are guilty of this without meaning to be. As Christians, we should never allow this to happen—but as humans, we do. Maybe it is only an attempt to bolster our egos, not intended to harm. When we treat another person with anything but love, we hurt only ourselves. It is not enough to be a Christian in our professed beliefs. We must be truly Christian in our words and deeds.

Dear Heavenly Father, help me to remember to treat others as I would like to be treated myself. Teach me to put the Golden Rule into practice at all times, and let me hold the attitude of prayer throughout each day, truthfully and sincerely.

3
Performance

Ability

PROVERBS 3:6 In everything you do, put God first, and he will direct you and crown your efforts with success.

THE ARCHERFISH

A jet of water hits the prey—
The archerfish has struck!
He has found his dinner,
With a little bit of luck.

He has the gift of shooting
Water from his mouth—
As straight as a tiny arrow,
Whether north, west, east, or south.

He seems to be an intelligent being,
For he works to improve his aim—
Sometimes it's used for dinner,
And sometimes just for a game.

The archerfish is found from India through Southeast Asia, the Malay Archipelago, and from Australia to the Philippines. Although it resides in brackish waters, it is also found in fresh water or in the sea. This little fish, up to a foot in length, has the uncanny ability to shoot down bugs with a stream of water from its mouth. It positions itself almost vertically in the water to lessen the refraction and then shoots from underneath the prey. It is very careful of how it directs that stream of water. If we only ask, God will direct our life stream, and just as the archerfish is rewarded with its dinner, our efforts will be crowned with success in the Lord. We must remember that the Lord directs—but we provide the effort!

Dear Lord, I thank You for Your direction in my life. I pray that I may follow through with what You lay out for me. Thank You for the love and support You provide.

I CORINTHIANS 13:11,12a It's like this: when I was a child I spoke and thought and reasoned as a child does. But when I became a man my thoughts grew far beyond those of my childhood, and now I have put away the childish things. In the same way, we can see and understand only a little about God now, as if we were peering at his reflection in a poor mirror; but someday we are going to see him in his completeness, face to face.

THE AXOLOTL

The strange axolotl,
Though sexually adult,
Usually stays a juvenile,
With a strange result.

It is a newt-like creature,
Amphibian by birth,
And yet some stay waterbound,
And never find their worth.

They become salamanders
Only if forced to be,
To live as adults upon the land—
Not larvae in the sea.

The axolotl is sometimes called the Peter Pan of the amphibian world. The adults can live in water or on the land, but the young—the larvae—are confined to the water. The strange thing about the axolotl is that it can spend its full life cycle in the larval state. Sometimes we may find ourselves in a similar position when we cling to an outlook gone stale and are fearful to venture into new mental and spiritual challenges. We miss so much of God's offerings when we fail to reach out and grow! Life is meant to be a continuous growing process. God expects it of us. Let's try to expect it of ourselves and put our hearts into working toward that end.

Dear Heavenly Father, I pray that I may continue to grow in knowledge and wisdom. What great opportunities You offer me for my betterment! As I strive to grow, increase my capacity for growth that I may follow Your Word with ever-deepening understanding.

PROVERBS 29:23 Pride ends in a fall, while humility brings honor.

THE BIRD OF PARADISE

The bird of paradise can be
Many different colors.
There are several species—
Each is different from the others.

They range from just five inches long
To almost thirty-eight.
Some are rather plain,
But most of them are quite ornate.

The male displays his feathers bright,
Bowing to show his crown.
Some species are peculiar,
And display hanging upside down.

They dance and sway and posture
To attract a future mate.
When mating time is over,
The displays soon abate!

The bird of paradise is closely related to the bowerbird. It has stout legs and feet and a heavy bill. It is found in New Guinea and in Australia, and also in offshore islands in those areas. It feeds on fruit and insects, with an occasional lizard or other small animal for an additional treat. It is truly proud of its plumage and shows it to great advantage. Sometimes we tend to be somewhat like the bird of paradise. We are tempted to show off in one way or another. Our possessions—abilities—knowledge—talents. It is here that the devil nudges us and uses the sin of pride. Let us remember that undue pride in self brings destruction—but joyous pride in our God brings humility.

Dear Father in Heaven, I pray that I may always remember that without You, I would be as nothing. I would have nothing. You created all—and all that I have and all that I am is Yours, dear Lord.

II CORINTHIANS 5:17 When someone becomes a Christian he becomes a brand new person inside. He is not the same any more. A new life has begun!

THE BUTTERFLY

Behold the beautiful butterfly
As he unfolds his wings.
Of all of God's creations,
He's one of the greatest things.

For he begins as a caterpillar
Crawling on Mother Earth,
And he ascends a butterfly—
The picture of rebirth.

For such a lowly worm was I
Before He picked me up.
Now I too have been reborn,
And drink from His flowing cup!

There are many species of butterflies that add beauty to our world. Each of these gorgeous creatures went through a transformation—from caterpillar to pupa, from pupa to butterfly. When we become Christians, we also go through a transformation. As the caterpillar sloughs off its old skin, so we—through God's grace—slough off our sinful self, and just as the butterfly emerges in all its beauty, so do we emerge as newborn creatures in Christ Jesus.

Dear Lord, what a vivid example of beauty and grace You have given us in the butterfly! Help me to steep my days in equal beauty by mirroring the Holy Spirit that dwells within.

PSALMS 24:1 The earth belongs to God! Everything in all the world is his!

THE CANADIAN LYNX

*The Canadian lynx is quite a cat—
A crafty hunter too.
He lives up in the north land
Where the mountains he can view.*

*He's well equipped to stand the cold,
He wears a heavy coat.
His big feet are like snowshoes,
And his eyes are worth a note.*

*They work so very well to see
That he can hunt at night.
He has no trouble finding food
If the conditions are just right.*

*He's three feet long from head to rear,
And often two feet high.
He has a beard and stubby tail,
And a caterwauling cry.*

*He really is a handsome beast,
And so light on his feet!
This crafty cat, the Canadian lynx,
Is a dangerous foe to meet!*

The lynx is indeed well equipped by its Creator. It is a pale brownish-gray, and its fur is more than an inch thick in the wintertime. Even its long legs are protected by this heavy blanket. It is an excellent climber and spends much of its time in trees. God has truly given it all that is needed for survival. It has but to use the gifts at its disposal. We too are well equipped if we but use the gifts that God has given us. He provides the means, but we must do our part and use them.

Dear Lord, help me to use to the best of my ability all the opportunities that You provide for me. I pray that I might step forth on faith and live my life for You.

I CORINTHIANS 12:4,5 Now God gives us many kinds of special abilities, but it is the same Holy Spirit who is the source of them all. There are different kinds of service to God, but it is the same Lord we are serving.

THE DODO BIRD

Funny little dodo bird,
What happened to your kind?
A cousin of the pigeon and dove,
But no longer can we find
This strange example of nature—
A bird who never flew,
But lived its life out on the ground,
Trying to hide from view!

And how about you? Today the dodo bird is extinct and has been for two hundred years or so. Do you suppose it is because it did not use its full potential? It is a medical fact that if we do not use our muscles, they will atrophy and wither. It is the same with our spiritual and mental "muscles." When we use them, their capacity increases and we enjoy their full benefit. When they are allowed to fall into disuse, they dry up and disappear. Let's not be like the dodo bird. Let's use our full potential. God expects it of us . . . He deserves it . . . and so do we!

Dear Heavenly Father, please help me to use the talents and abilities that You have given me. Help me to stay on a spiritual and mental exercise program that will keep me alert and in touch with Your love.

I CORINTHIANS 12:1 And now, brothers, I want to write about the special abilities the Holy Spirit gives to each of you, for I don't want any misunderstanding about them.

THE GECKO LIZARD

Gecko lizards love to climb
Wherever they are found.
They have the strange ability
To scamper upside down.

The feet are covered with friction pads
With many little discs
That act like tiny suction cups,
So the geckos take no risks.

They move across the ceiling
As easily as can be.
There really are no limits
To their mobility.

The gecko lizards live in swamps, forests, and deserts—on mountains and on islands—anyplace where the nights are not too cold. They range from two inches to a foot in length, and half of that is tail. Their feet are composed of four enlarged toes, each equipped with a suction grip of multitudinous bristles. They move with a peculiar gait, as the toes must be curled up with each step to disengage the grip. The gecko has a special ability that allows it to not only climb a pane of glass but to scamper across the ceiling as easily as across the sand. Each of us has a special ability too. It may be the ability to comfort, to counsel, to write, to sing, or to paint—any one of innumerable talents. Since it takes many talents to further God's Kingdom, we cannot expect to have the same abilities as our neighbors and our friends. We must each find our own unique talent and then develop it for God—and for our own edification.

Dear Heavenly Father, I praise You for giving me a talent. Help me to search until I find it. Then teach me to work hard with the Spirit to develop it that I may use it for Your Kingdom.

PROVERBS 24:3,4 Any enterprise is built by wise planning, becomes strong through common sense, and profits wonderfully by keeping abreast of the facts.

THE HORNET

A hornet's nest is quite unique,
Constructed carefully.
They choose human neighbors,
And hang their nest from eave or tree.

They chew woody plant material
And mix it with their spit
To produce a paper product,
And build their nests with it.

The hornet is a species of wasp,
But it is large in size.
It uses its God-given talents well—
We should be as wise!

The hornet is a species of wasp. Most wasps build their homes in the ground, but the hornet prefers a higher location, preferably around human dwellings. It uses wise planning in its building, calling upon its unique ability to create building material. The hornet truly profits by using its knowledge and instincts. We can build a strong and profitable life if we use all our capabilities for Christ. Any enterprise we may enter into will prosper if we let the Spirit lead and use for the Lord's Glory the talents He has given us. With His Word as our blueprint, we can build our lives on the sturdy foundation of His love.

Dear Lord, I pray that I may make the very best use of the knowledge and common sense You have given me. Help me each day to find my purpose in Your service. I love You and praise You for Your faith in me—may I never be a disappointment to You.

PROVERBS 22:17–19 Listen to this wise advice; follow it closely, for it will do you good, and you can pass it on to others: *Trust in the Lord.*

THE LONG-EARED JERBOA

This jerboa lives in Mongolia,
A rodent with extra-big ears.
His hind legs are extremely long,
And his prodigious leaps merit cheers.

He has a rather piglike snout,
With whiskers that reach to his tail.
He really isn't very big,
But strange-looking, without fail.

His fur is soft and silky,
And colored like the sand.
His tail is long and very thin,
And adorned with a wide black band.

Jerboas range in size from one and a half inches to six inches in length. The long-eared jerboas fall somewhere in-between. They are desert animals, primarily nocturnal in nature. They have quite elaborate burrows, with nest chambers and multiple entrances. The ears of this little creature are rabbit-sized. It must make very good use of them! Indeed, we need to make good use of our ears too. They may not be as big, but they are certainly as important. It is through our ears that we hear the Gospel for the first time, and our hearing is important in increasing our knowledge. It helps us to be cognizant of the joys and sorrows of those around us, and if we use our hearing so that we *really* listen, we find that we are using our hearts as well as our ears!

Dear Lord, help me to keep my ears open to what is going on around me. Help me to be wise too, so that my reactions to what I hear will be in Your service. I pray that I may use wisdom in divining the words I hear and that I may accept the truth and reject the false.

MATTHEW 7:21 Not all who sound religious are really godly people. They may refer to me as "Lord", but still won't get to heaven. For the decisive question is whether they obey my Father in heaven.

THE OARFISH

Tales of strange sea creatures
Have been told down through the years.
The oarfish could be the reason
For many a sailor's fears.

He may be twenty feet in length
With a coral dorsal fin
That stands straight up from head to tail,
And he's seldom seen by men.

He's only two inches wide at most,
And about twelve inches tall.
When seen close to the surface,
He doesn't look like a fish at all!

This strange-looking fish has a crest at the front of the dorsal fin and bright, coral-red pelvic fins that are long and slender—oar-shaped—from which its name is derived. It may also be called the ribbonfish. The oarfish has a very small mouth and no teeth. It has forty-two to fifty-eight gill rakers to strain extra-small crustaceans from the water as it passes over the gills. It seems that an oarfish can lose the rear half of its body and yet survive because all the internal organs are packed in the front. Just as people may sometimes see the oarfish surface and mistake it for a sea monster, so we may sometimes listen to speakers who dazzle us with empty words. We must be very careful not to be led astray by false promises but to test others' words by God's Word. In this way we not only use our faith, we strengthen it as we increase our dependency on Him Who guides us so surely.

Dear Heavenly Father, give me the gift of discernment that I might be able to tell the true from the false. I know that I must look beyond mere appearances, for appearances can be deceiving. Help me to use Your teachings that I may grow in wisdom and knowledge.

EPHESIANS 4:11 Some of us have been given special ability as apostles; to others he has given the gift of being able to preach well; some have special ability in winning people to Christ, helping them to trust him as their Savior; still others have a gift for caring for God's people as a shepherd does his sheep, leading and teaching them in the ways of God.

THE OCELOT

The ocelot is a beautiful cat.
He's muscular and seldom fat.
This animal climbs with a great skill,
But stalks his prey to make a kill.
He's greatly prized for his gorgeous coat,
And here's an interesting thing to note—
No two are alike—each one is unique.
They may be marked with spot, ring, or streak.
They are small and easily tamed, they say,
And that makes them a threatened species today.

The ocelot is not very large—twenty-five to thirty-five pounds—and feeds on snakes, lizards, and small or medium-sized mammals. The ocelot's coat is beautiful in its very uniqueness. We too are truly unique. We each belong to the same human species, and yet no two of us are exactly alike. We may have different colors of skin and hair, and different features—but we are all from the same family. As Christians, we have received special talents and abilities from God, and my talents and abilities may be very different from yours. Together, though, they are a part of the whole that we share. A Christian never envies another Christian or wishes for his talent. Instead, he finds and develops his own. Yes, we are each unique—there's no one else exactly like you! Isn't that fantastic? Nobody can make your contribution to mankind but *you!*

Dear Heavenly Father, I thank You for creating me—for giving me the opportunity to grow and develop and contribute in my own unique way. I thank You that I, like the ocelot, am different and not a duplicate of someone else. Help me to cherish that difference and to use it to Your advantage.

I CORINTHIANS 12:27 Now here is what I am trying to say: All of you together are the one body of Christ and each one of you is a separate and necessary part of it.

THE OWL

The owl is something special—
He's different far, you see.
His senses are quite intricate
And work quite gloriously.

For one, his eyes are mighty,
Seeing the tiniest thing.
Although they don't move in their sockets,
They're strong as anything!

His ears are full of power;
His hearing is long-range.
He uses his ears in hunting prey,
And that will never change.

His feathers are soft and fluffy—
He doesn't make a sound.
His talons are long and deadly sharp
To catch prey when it's found.

Yes, the owl abounds in gifts for its survival, and it uses each of them. They all work together. How would it survive if it lost its hearing?—or its sight?—or its strong talons? All of them are needed. The church is much the same. Each one of us has a different talent, but we all are needed to make an effective witness for Christ. The church is the body of Christ, and we as individuals are only parts of that body. Come, let us work together—as God intended us to.

Dear Heavenly Father, I praise You for allowing me to be a part of the body of Christ. Help me to do my job, to use my talents, and to assist in keeping that body healthy and in good working order.

PROVERBS 22:3 A prudent man foresees the difficulties ahead and prepares for them; the simpleton goes blindly on and suffers the consequences.

THE SEA HORSE

The sea horse is an amazing creature
In appearance and in acts.
He's the stallion of the waters,
And I'll share with you some facts.

His eyes are wonderful to see,
For they turn in different ways.
He can watch above and under,
And for him, that really pays.

He has the power to camouflage
With a color-changing coat.
If prizes were given for oddities,
The sea horse would certainly get my vote!

The sea horse is indeed an oddity. The female courts the male, and he carries her eggs in a little pouch, releasing baby "sea colts" after forty-five days of waiting. Since the sea horses' eyes are independent of each other, they can look both ahead and behind at the same time. Indeed we can too, in our own way. We can look ahead toward the future and behind at the past. We can learn from our mistakes, and try not to repeat them. Just as the sea horse's vision works for the sea horse, so our spiritual vision works for us.

Dear Lord, thank You for Your many blessings. I pray that I might use "double vision," looking behind myself in order to better see ahead. Give me the wisdom to use my past experience in making my future decisions.

PSALMS 86:11 Tell me where you want me to go and I will go there. May every fiber of my being unite in reverence to your name.

THE SPIDER

Silver cobwebs in the sun,
Spinning, spinning, one by one.
The spider works his whole life through
Spinning cobwebs in the dew.

From slender stalk to treetop high
He's spinning, spinning to the sky,
Doing what God would have him do
Can you say as much for you?

Have you ever watched a little web-spinning spider at work? It can do the impossible, it seems. So tiny, yet it can spin untold yards of beautiful, delicate webbing. It is doing what God equipped it to do. And what about us? Are we using our talents for God? Are we doing what He wants us to do—going where He wants us to go?

Dear Lord, help us to use the tiny spider as an object lesson. You have given each of us special talents and special abilities. Help us to find them and use them before it is too late.

EPHESIANS 3:20 Now glory be to God who by his mighty power at work within us is able to do far more than we would ever dare to ask or even dream of—infinitely beyond our highest prayers, desires, thoughts, or hopes.

THE SUGARBIRD

The sugarbird lives in Africa
Among the protea shrub—
He rarely leaves his habitat,
And therein lies the rub!

He has a strange dependence
On the protea bush, you see—
He depends on it for insects,
For nesting and nectar honey.

He will not leave the protea shrubs
Unless a food shortage occurs
And forces him to move away
To another protea—strange bird!

The sugarbird may be seventeen inches long, but twelve inches of this length is its flowing tail. The bill is long and slightly curved downward. It is equipped to live on insects and nectar. Why this strange dependence on the protea shrubs? The sugarbird could very well find the same insects on other plants, and nectar as well, but it is conditioned to stay with the protea. Many of us are somewhat similar. We prefer the familiar and shy away from the strange. Change upsets us. Oh, the things we may be missing! "I can't do this," or "I wouldn't dare try that." How many times do we hear such statements—or, indeed, make them ourselves? Yet if we open up to God, He can use us in ways we never thought possible! Reach for your dreams—pray for Him to use you, and you just might be surprised at the results.

Dear Heavenly Father, I know that You will work through me, if I will just allow it. Help me to shed my doubts and fears and give myself completely over to Your leading. I wait, Lord, with bated breath for the results in my life. I love You and praise You!

Action

MATTHEW 13:20,21 The shallow, rocky soil represents the heart of a man who hears the message and receives it with real joy, but he doesn't have much depth in his life, and the seeds don't root very deeply, and after a while when trouble comes, or persecution begins because of his beliefs, his enthusiasm fades, and he drops out.

THE ADDAX

There've been pictures of the addax
For forty-five hundred years.
From the antelope family,
He has big horns and ears.

The horns grow in a spiral
And are beautiful to see—
His hide is used for shoe leather
And commands an exorbitant fee.

An addax isn't hard to catch—
He expends his energy fast
Instead of spreading it over time,
And trying to make it last.

The addax is a species of antelope. Today it is found from Algeria to the Sudan. The ancient Egyptians had it semi-domesticated, and it was quite a status symbol. It has become increasingly rare because of its beautiful horns and strong hide. Hunters find it easy game because it exhausts itself so quickly. The addax expends all of its energy at one burst and is soon too spent to defend itself. Some people react in the same way. At first they accept the Gospel with enormous enthusiasm, but—like the energy of the addax—that enthusiasm soon wanes. The steps of the Christian are not meant to be taken all at one time. Rather, each step is one part of a journey toward our Lord that calls on us for steadfastness and perseverance. Let's not be like the addax!

Dear Lord, I pray that I may send my roots deep into Your Word and live my Christian witness at a steady pace, always looking to You and ever open to the Spirit's leading. Help me to realize, Lord, that life cannot be a constant high and that I must go down into the plains and valleys too. With You to guide me, I pray that I may steadily follow in Your footsteps.

PROVERBS 6:6 Take a lesson from the ants, you lazy fellow. Learn from their ways and be wise!

THE ANT

The lowly little crawling ants—
Workers tried and true!
There are many different kinds,
But all have the same view—

That life and work go hand in hand,
And they must ever be
Going about their daily job
Of building the family.

There are carpenters and farmers,
Soldiers and sailors too.
Steamship ants, and parasols,
Just to name a few!

There are many different types of ant tribes, and they pursue occupations very much like those of the human race. No wonder Solomon chose to use them as a lesson in Proverbs! You cannot study an anthill, or even a single ant, without being amazed at their activity. They are constantly busy—constantly on the go. They keep food in the larder, and none go hungry. If one job is finished, they find another task to complete. Busy hands cannot get into trouble. If we keep busy too, how much happier we are! What a shame it is to waste a single precious moment of our time on earth. This does not mean that we should be busy *all* the time—some of our finest ideas come when we take "time out"—but that we learn to control our use of the time the Lord has given us, and not just fritter it away.

Dear Lord, please help me to take a lesson from the ant and use my time to advantage. Help me to generate enthusiasm and use the abilities You have provided me with. I pray that I might contribute something worthwhile and that I will hear You say, "My child, well done," at the close of this earthly existence.

II THESSALONIANS 3:10 Even while we were still there with you we gave you this rule: "He who does not work shall not eat."

THE BEAVER

"Busy as a beaver"
Is a saying old and true.
"Why is a beaver busy?"
Is the question I ask you.

He's a woodcutter and architect,
A mason and builder supreme.
He's really quite a lumberjack—
A tree makes his eyes gleam.

He's busy, busy, busy,
And can help or hinder man—
According to where he works,
And where he decides to build a dam.

He has a reason for working so hard—
He gnaws and gnaws on a tree,
For if he doesn't, his incisors grow
And he can't close his mouth, you see!

Maybe we should have incentive such as the beaver has! Truly, the beaver is a worker, but maybe that is because it instinctively knows that if it does not work and keep its gnawing teeth filed down, it will be unable to eat. If we do not work, or if we become lazy, we may still be able to eat, but we will starve spiritually. We cannot practice laziness and Christianity at the same time. We cannot feed on the Word of God without wanting to take action. Laziness has no place in our walk with God for He enjoins us to act with compassion, to speak with love, and to give with charity. Yes, a Christian is as "busy as a beaver!"

Dear Lord, please help me to stay active, both physically and spiritually. I may have limitations laid on me, but help me to do as much as You have equipped me to do. Help me to find my incentive in You.

I PETER 2:15 It is God's will that your good lives should silence those who foolishly condemn the Gospel without knowing what it can do for them, having never experienced its power.

THE CARDINAL

A bunting called the cardinal
Has plumage of bright red.
He has a facial mask of black
And a crest upon his head.

Some people call him "redbird."
His bill is strong and stout.
His food consists of berries
And seeds he finds about.

His song is really not the best,
But he's a beautiful bird,
And to see him fly to a tree nearby
Is a sermon without a word.

Yes, the cardinal is a welcome sight. Its very presence seems to fill our hearts with wonder at God's Creation and make the unbeliever stop to think. Our lives should speak out a sermon too. By observing the life of a Christian, many an unbeliever has been changed. We should always be aware that someone is watching and that we are constantly witnessing in one way or another—either for or against Christ. There is no sitting on the fence!

Dear Heavenly Father, I pray that my life might be a good witness for You and that it might create a hunger in others for Your peace—the peace given us by You and Your great sacrifice on the cross at Calvary. Let me, like the cardinal, shine out to those around me, reflecting Your Glory!

EPHESIANS 6:5-8 Slaves, obey your masters; be eager to give them your very best. Serve them as you would Christ. Don't work hard only when your master is watching and then shirk when he isn't looking; work hard and with gladness all the time, as though working for Christ, doing the will of God with all your hearts. Remember the Lord will pay you for each good thing you do, whether you are slave or free.

THE CORMORANT

In China and Japan, they use
The cormorant to work.
They put a ring around his neck,
He has no chance to shirk!

They put him out to catch the fish
The ring won't let him eat.
The fishermen's business may be good,
But the cormorant feels defeat!

He is worthy of his hire,
And he is treated well.
He does a good job catching fish
For the fishermen to sell.

The cormorant is a long-necked, long-billed diving bird. It is also called a shag. There are thirty known species. About fifty percent of the cormorant's catch is marketable size and nature, so it has been much persecuted by fishermen through the years. However, for centuries some of the men of China and Japan have taken advantage of the cormorant's ability and used it to catch fish for them, afterward rewarding the bird with the less-valuable fish caught. The cormorants made good "slaves," or "servants." We are all "slaves" in one sense of the word. We must work to make our living—and most of us work for someone else. It is sometimes tempting to slack off and shirk our duties, to do less than our best. Work becomes tedious and tiresome. But we must remember that everything we do—*everything*—is a witness for or against Christ, and we are obligated to do our very best! After all, the primary "boss" is God—and it is He Who will judge whether or not we have been good workers. It's true—our work attitudes may lead another soul to Christ—or away from Him.

Dear Heavenly Father, thank You for giving me the ability to do the tasks You assign. Help me to do my very best—cheerfully and willingly—in everything I do.

PROVERBS 16:26,27 Hunger is good—if it makes you work to satisfy it! Idle hands are the devil's workshop; idle lips are his mouthpiece.

THE ELEPHANT SHREW

If you can imagine a mouse with a trunk,
Or even a rat—it is true,
You'll get half a picture of a strange little creature
Named the elephant shrew.

His proboscis is long and pointed,
And the reason's not just chance.
It's so that he can nose out food—
Termites, bugs, and ants.

There are fifteen different species,
And most are brown or gray—
One group within the forest, though,
Is patterned to hide away.

Although elephant shrews are found mostly in Africa, one species is found in Morocco and Algeria. They have a long and pointed proboscis, which is a great help in obtaining food. They have a long, naked tail and large, bright eyes. Their build is much like that of the normal mouse or rat. Their coat color usually matches the surrounding soil and serves to camouflage them from predators. They are a daytime creature, and their favorite food seems to be termites, ants, and other insects. They must go out and forage for food to appease their hunger. We also must work to satisfy our hunger—not only our hunger for food but for the very meaning of life. When we find that meaning in God's Word, we will be compelled all the more strongly to spread the Good News to others. Truly, a Christ-directed life is a busy life, with no room for the devil!

Dear Lord, I pray that I may keep my hands, heart, and lips busy proclaiming the Gospel message. There is a hunger, an empty place, in our lives until Your Word is heard. Help me to stay busy proclaiming You, Lord. I thank You and praise You for all You have done for me.

I CORINTHIANS 16:13 Keep your eyes open for spiritual danger; stand true to the Lord; act like men; be strong; and whatever you do, do it with kindness and love.

THE FOUR-EYED FISH

With two eyes divided,
The four-eyed fish has four.
Central America is his habitat,
And he swims there, along the shore.

Two eyes see above the water,
And two eyes see below—
They cruise along, looking up and down,
Watching for food or foe.

The four-eyed fish are freshwater toothcarps found in Central America. They are of the family *Anablepidae*. Their eyes are really only two, but each is divided horizontally into two distinct parts. The upper half is equipped for vision in the air and the lower half for vision in the water. The lens is different in each half. The fish cruises along at the water line, where it can see both above and below the water as it watches for food, and also for predators. It has no tear ducts and so must duck its head to prevent its "air eyes" from drying out. It also keeps its eyes open for danger. We too must keep our eyes open—both our physical eyes and the eyes of the heart. Sometimes we see with the heart things that are closed to our physical eyes. Seeing must precede action, for how can we know what action to take unless we have viewed the situation—in one way or the other?

Dear Lord, please help me to remain alert and to keep both my physical and spiritual eyes open to the life around me. Then help me to act on what I see with kindness and love.

PROVERBS 21:20 The wise man saves for the future, but the foolish man spends whatever he gets.

THE GRAY SQUIRREL

The friendly little gray squirrel
With the bushy tail
Is a busy creature—
As through the leaves he sails.

He leaps and scampers up a tree,
Always on the run.
If he's not really working,
Then he's just having fun.

He's really quite intelligent,
And stores his food away
Until he really needs it,
When winter's here to stay.

The little gray squirrel is a delightful animal to watch. It is quick, smart, and industrious. The squirrel's greatest asset seems to be its tail. He grooms it and uses it constantly. It is protection from the cold and rain, a parachute when falling, a soft landing, and very attractive too! The squirrel is always on the go. Since it seems to want to squeeze every moment out of life, it will waste nothing. It may store several thousand nuts away during the fall in order to have a good supply for the winter months. We can take a lesson from this intelligent little creature and save a portion of what we receive. We must not hoard or be selfish, but we must be good stewards of the bounty the Lord provides—and surely all that we obtain is provided by Him!

Dear Lord, thank You for providing for my needs. Help me to be a good steward of all I am entrusted with. I love You and praise You, Lord, for Your mercy and love.

I CORINTHIANS 15:58 So, my dear brothers, since future victory is sure, be strong and steady, always abounding in the Lord's work, for you know that nothing you do for the Lord is ever wasted as it would be if there were no resurrection.

THE HUMMINGBIRD

Pretty little hummingbird
Sipping from a flower,
Spreading pollen here and there,
Sipping, sipping, by the hour.

Working out His purpose,
In God's world you abide—
Spreading plants and flowers,
Pollinating the countryside.

You give us quite a picture
Of our purpose here on earth,
Spreading Jesus' Gospel
And the glory of "new birth."

New birth in Christ Jesus—
For those who haven't heard—
Helps us do our very best,
As the little hummingbird.

The hummingbird is a quandary to me. It's so tiny, and yet one small hummingbird can chase off a good-sized hawk. It can travel amazingly fast and is highly aggressive, although the smallest of the species is only two inches long, tail and all. How effective it is for its size! Often we hear, "I can't do anything—I'm only one person." We should be ashamed! One person can work miracles if he lets the Lord work through him and does his best, as the little hummingbird does.

Dearest Lord, help me to open myself to You and Your Word. Help me to fulfill my purpose, just as the hummingbird does. And may I have the confidence to realize that I can be effective, to know that with Your Spirit within me, I too can work miracles in Your Name.

GALATIANS 5:13 For, dear brothers, you have been given freedom: not freedom to do wrong, but freedom to love and serve each other.

THE LADYBIRD BEETLE

These tiny ladybird beetles
Have played an important part
In the raising of our grain foods
From the very start.

They were brought from Australia
To control the scale insects.
South Africa also used them,
When they saw the beetles' effects.

We hail the beetles' presence,
And children everywhere
Have wished the "ladybug" Godspeed
As she travels through the air.

Many countries have discovered the value of this little six-legged creature in controlling destructive pests. It is probably one of our greatest allies in the field of agriculture. The ladybug truly serves humankind! We have the freedom in Christ to truly serve one another too. There is a great joy in service that is hard to understand before we ourselves have experienced it. Have you tried it? If not, do, and then you will know the joy of the freedom Christ gives in service.

Dear Lord, help me to use my freedom wisely. I pray that I might be humble enough to serve others with joy and love, giving of myself without thought of return, and revealing Your Spirit in my every action and way.

PROVERBS 27:12 A sensible man watches for problems ahead and prepares to meet them. The simpleton never looks, and suffers the consequences.

THE MUSKRAT

Some people call the muskrat
The beaver's little brother.
He's closer to a meadow mouse,
But they resemble one another.

The muskrat is much smaller,
And he doesn't harvest trees.
He builds his house of cattails,
Or he builds his house of reeds.

His name is due to a gland
That gives a musky smell.
He is a graceful, active swimmer,
And a land animal as well.

The muskrat is a quiet animal, and most of its activity takes place at night. It spends much of its life in the water, and its house is built with several underwater entrances. It is a good, clean housekeeper. It even builds a private dining room, a small hut where it can eat in peace without worrying about predators. What a smart animal, this little muskrat! It truly prepares to meet its problems before they arrive. If we would only do the same! It is so easy to ignore the little things until they have grown big enough to be problems.

Lord, help me to grow in wisdom, to be sensible enough to foresee the problems that might lie ahead, and to prepare for them. The future is in Your hands, but I know that I am responsible for doing my part too!

PROVERBS 20:6 Most people will tell you what loyal friends they are, but are they telling the truth?

THE PIED WAGTAIL

*The very name, "pied wagtail,"
May bring a smile or grin,
But the bird that bears that funny name
Is something else again.*

*The wagtail feasts on flies and such,
And uses various ways
To get her food and feed her chicks—
She's found that friendship pays.*

*She may form a partnership
With a fallow deer—
She plucks the flies that bother him,
And has no cause to fear.*

*Her babes may line up on his back
As she feeds them, one by one.
The deer is rid of biting pests,
And her feeding chores are done.*

The pied wagtail is almost entirely restricted to the Old World. It is a small bird whose food consists of small insects. It is a ground nester. Truly, it has found the value of working in harmony not only with its own kind, but with other creatures in God's world. Sometimes it takes man a long time to learn what the pied wagtail seems to know at birth!

Dear Lord, help me to be a loyal friend and to be always ready to help others. Words come easy, but the proof is in the action. I pray that my actions may be a positive witness for You and Your Word and that I may truly "do unto others."

PROVERBS 13:16 A wise man thinks ahead; a fool doesn't, and even brags about it!

THE POCKET GOPHER

This gopher lives in North America,
In arid regions where he wills.
A furry rodent, he lives alone
In the tunnels that he builds.

He has pouches in his cheeks,
And uses them to convey
Greens and roots and bulbs and such,
To his special hideaway.

He builds spacious chambers
To hold his food supply.
He plans for tomorrow,
And so should you and I!

Pocket gophers are from four to ten inches long and get their name from the large pouches on each cheek. These pouches open by a slit on the outside. They are lined with fur and can be turned inside out to empty their contents. The gopher fills them with bulbs and roots and green plants to store for future use. It constructs special storage chambers for these treasures. It truly looks ahead and plans for tomorrow. We would be wise to look ahead too and plan for the future. God will take care of us, but He certainly intends for us to do our part. Just as the little brown pocket gopher works hard to provide for its own, we should too. God tells us not to worry, but He doesn't tell us not to prepare.

Dear Heavenly Father, I pray that I might be wise enough to think ahead and be ready for whatever may come. I know I do not have to worry about the future, but help me to use the brainpower You have given me as it was intended to be used, that I may be prepared.

PROVERBS 10:4 Lazy men are soon poor; hard workers get rich.

THE RACCOON

The raccoon with black patches
Around his big, dark eyes,
Looks like a bandit;
He's also very wise.

His body is roly-poly,
And he eats quite a lot.
He'll raid a field or garbage can
Without a second thought.

He washes food before he eats;
He has no saliva glands.
He's a clever little creature,
And eats his food with his hands.

The raccoon is found throughout the United States and also in Mexico and Canada. It likes the marshes, streams, and woodlands. Since it really does not like work very much, it finds an abandoned burrow or hollow tree to call home. It is a little robber! If you have ever gone camping, you have probably heard it at night, popping garbage-can lids and getting into anything left out in the open. These scavenging ways may be all right for the raccoon, but certainly not for us. As the raccoon opts for lazy living, haphazard support, and cast-off housing, we feel a little sorry for it. It has nothing to really count on—no security. As Christians, we will work as God intended us to and earn the rich warmth of His love and grace. We can always count on Him, and we grow spiritually wealthy and secure in His Word.

Dear Lord, I thank You for Your love and care—for a roof over my head and food on my table. You always provide for my needs, and I am grateful for the opportunity to work for You. May I ever do my best, in Your Name.

JAMES 4:17 Remember, too, that knowing what is right to do and then not doing it is sin.

THE SEA GULL

Have you seen a sea gull
Gracefully glide
Over the water
With his mate by his side?

Dipping and sailing
Through the sky's blue,
It's a beautiful sight—
It does something to you.

The sun glistens brightly
On the span of his wing;
His symbol is purity—
He makes the heart sing.

The gull has at least forty-three species, but the herring gull, or sea gull, is the one we focus on here. The gull spends twenty-six days in the shell and twenty-four hours to break out to freedom. Then comes the crucial moment. The parent gull has a red spot on the underside of the beak. In order to get food, the little chick must tap this spot, causing the parent to choke up food with which to feed the new family addition. If the chick does not tap the red button, it may die of starvation. It knows what it must do, and if it does not do it, it starves. How like our own lives! Unless we open and study the Word of God, we will die of spiritual starvation. The end result would be death—eternally. But if we tap the Source, just as the young gull taps its source, we will be fed and nourished—to grow and thrive for ever.

Dear Lord, help me to tap the Source that I may drink from the Living Water and be fed from Your Word. I thank You for the example of the young sea gull, and I pray that I may constantly hold Your Word in my heart.

PROVERBS 10:26 A lazy fellow is a pain to his employers—like smoke in their eyes or vinegar that sets the teeth on edge.

THE SLOTH

The sloth is strange to ponder—
He hardly moves at all;
Hanging by his powerful claws,
You know he will not fall.

He feeds on leaves and flowers
High up in the trees.
He takes twelve days to move four miles—
He really takes his ease.

Now sloths are made to be lazy,
They know no other way—
But we are just the opposite;
We need to work each day!

The sloth is so quiet and immobile that tiny plants grow on its hair, which is coarse and dense. Caterpillars feed on the plants, and—lo and behold!—moths may be seen flying out of the untidy covering of the sloth. The four legs of this creature are so underdeveloped and weak from disuse that they cannot support the sloth's weight. As the sloth was made for "laziness," so humans are made for work. We need to be active for our own benefit—spiritually, mentally, and physically. As Christians, we are a unit, and we must each carry our share of the load. Have you ever worked beside someone who continually did less than his share of work? His behavior not only gave the rest of you more work to do, but it hurt him too, weakening his attitudes and his future ability to cope with responsibility.

Dear Lord, help me to carry my fair share and to not be "lazy" in my duties. Any job worth doing is worth doing well, and I pray that I may work up to my capabilities and never let my fellow workers down. Help my work attitudes to be a good witness for Christ.

MARK 13:35-37 Keep a sharp lookout! For you do not know when I will come, at evening, at midnight, early dawn or late daybreak. Don't let me find you sleeping. *Watch for my return!* This is my message to you and to everyone else.

THE STONE CURLEW

This wader has two names—
He's also called "thick knees"
Because of his swollen knee joints,
And there are nine species.

Although he is a wader,
He usually stays away
From the water—thus his name—
And he sleeps during the day.

At night he is quite noisy—
A "watchdog" he can be,
And many of the animals
Rely on his company!

The stone curlew, or "thick knees," ranges in size from fourteen to twenty-one inches long. The fairly long legs have slightly webbed feet with no hind toe. The curlew is gray, with black and brown streaks. Although it is a wader, it usually is found a way from the water. It is nocturnal and hides during the day. It is a great "watchman," and many animals, including the crocodile and the hippo, respond to its warnings. In South America, it is often tamed by the local people to act as a "watchman." It keeps a sharp lookout—and so should we! As we wait for the Lord's return, we must be diligent and continue our work. Let us be busy for the Kingdom when He comes!

Dear Heavenly Father, I wait with excitement and joy for the return of Your dear Son. I pray that I might keep a good watch and not become lax with the passing of time. I want to make every moment count!

4
Praise

PSALMS 148:5–7 Let everything he has made give praise to him. For he issued his command, and they came into being; he established them forever and forever. His orders will never be revoked. And praise him down here on earth, you creatures of the ocean depths.

THE ABALONE

The "ear shell," or abalone,
Has a single shell
Of iridescent beauty—
People know it well!

Found in California,
Along the coastline there,
The red, the green, the black one—
Although the black one's rare.

This creature has a foot
That people like to eat.
It is a delicacy,
This abalone meat.

The abalone is a gastropod mollusk. The shell is very beautiful, with iridescent colors on the inside, and on the outside too, when the surface is polished. A large, muscular foot attached to the shell is eaten as a delicacy. The foot anchors the abalone to a rock, and a number of perforations on the side of the shell allow the water to emerge after passing the creature's gills. The red abalone grows to ten inches across, the green up to six inches, and the black up to five inches. The black abalone differs from the others; it lives in the surf and consequently has a shining, clean shell. As the muscular foot of the abalone anchors it to the rock, let us also be anchored to our Rock, Jesus Christ! As the colors of the abalone shell praise God, let us praise Him with our lives.

Dear Father in Heaven, help me to sing praises to Jesus, my Rock in this sea of life. As the abalone is anchored to its rock, so I am anchored to You. May I always reflect Your Glory in all that I do and say.

JOHN 10:14,15 I am the Good Shepherd and know my own sheep, and they know me, just as my Father knows me and I know the Father; and I lay down my life for the sheep.

THE BARRACUDA

In the waters of the tropics
The barracuda swims.
A relative of the mullet,
His teeth identify him.

He may act as a shepherd
To the fish he will attack.
He is a fierce predator—
Fear won't turn him back.

He has injured divers
In the West Indies sea,
But in the Hawaiian Islands
He's harmless as can be.

Along the East Coast, the smallest of the barracuda grows to about eighteen inches in length, but the great barracuda—found in the western Pacific and on both sides of the tropical Atlantic—can grow to eight feet in length. In the West Indies it is a known hazard to divers, but in Hawaii it has the reputation of being harmless to man. The reason for the difference is a mystery. The barracuda uses a shepherding technique to capture its prey, shepherding it like a sheep to the slaughter. Praise the Lord that He shepherds us with love and care, and not to a slaughter but to eternal life! He truly is the Good Shepherd, and He laid down His life for us, His sheep.

Dear Lord, thank You for caring so much for me. I am glad to be in Your "sheepfold" and to be guided by such a loving Shepherd. Help me, Lord, to do my share by guiding others to You.

JAMES 1:21 So get rid of all that is wrong in your life, both inside and outside, and humbly be glad for the wonderful message we have received, for it is able to save our souls as it takes hold of our hearts.

THE BISON

The Old West brings memories
Of Indians brave and strong.
They hunted the shaggy bison
Just to get along.

They ate the meat and used the hide
For clothing and a tent.
They respected the bison—
They knew how much he meant.

With the coming of the railroad,
The bison herds grew small.
As time went by, these creatures
Were hardly seen at all.

The herds are growing larger now,
As the bison are raised
In a controlled environment,
Where once the wild herds grazed.

The wild bison were a main source of meat and skins for the Indian. Although big and strong, it was in constant danger of death by man, wolves, and other predators. Today it is able to graze openly and unafraid in a protected environment. So we once lived in sin, in constant danger of losing our very souls. Now, with the protection of the Holy Spirit, we can live with peace in our hearts, knowing that Jesus Christ conquered sin and death for all who accept Him as Lord. Praise God for His grace!

Dear Heavenly Father, I thank You for rescuing me from the constant battle with sin and Satan. I can live with peace in my heart, knowing that You are my protection and that You are truly in control. I am free of Satan, secure in Your love.

I JOHN 2:29 Since we know that God is always good and does only right, we may rightly assume that all those who do right are his children.

THE BITTERLING

An example of cooperation
Comes from the ocean deep.
The bitterling, a carplike fish,
A true partnership will seek.

First she finds a mussel
And lays her eggs inside;
In exchange, the mussel larvae
Upon the fish will ride.

The mussel releases the little fish—
The mussel larvae will grow,
And leave the female bitterling
For the freshwater depths below.

This magnificent example of cooperation in nature is a mystery to man. Why does it happen, and how does it work? The results are obvious. When God created, He created without any loose ends. As the mussel shell protects the eggs of the bitterling, so the mussel larvae are protected as they attach to the fish. It is as God intended. God is always good and does only right! As His children, we have the assurance that with His guidance and direction, we too are equipped to do right. Let us strive toward that goal and do our very best to carry His banner high. We belong to the King of kindness!

Dear Heavenly Father, I thank You and praise You for the assurance that You will always be there to counsel and guide me should I stumble, that You will pick me up should I fall, brush me off, and help me start again. Truly, You are good and right!

DANIEL 2:20 Blessed be the name of God forever and ever, for he alone has all wisdom and all power.

THE CHEVROTAIN

The chevrotain, or mouse deer
As he's called due to his size,
Has a small head and slender legs,
And is credited for being wise.

This tiny deer is one foot high,
And marked with spots and stripes.
He can't be classified a true deer,
And the family contains four types—

The Indian spotted chevrotain,
The Larger and Lesser Malay,
And then the Water chevrotain
From Africa across the way.

We call it local folklore,
But the natives say they possess
Unusual powers of reasoning
And can lead you to success.

The chevrotain are the smallest ruminants known in the world today. They are approximately a foot high at the shoulder and have no horns or antlers. They have four toes and walk on the tips of the hoofs. They swim, dive, and can climb a tree if the trunk is sufficiently sloped. They rest during the day and feed at night. They are found in forest, jungle, or scrub—sometimes in outlying gardens of the villages. They are very shy and run alone except for pairing during the breeding season. This tiny, deerlike animal has probably changed very little in the last few million years. The local people in Africa and Asia feel the chevrotain possesses unusual powers of wisdom. We know better. True, they have the knowledge necessary to survive, but they cannot impart that to us. Only God can!

Dear Lord, truly I know that You are the Source of all wisdom and power. I pray that You may equip me with what I need for living a Christian life in this troubled old world of ours.

PSALMS 108:1 O God, my heart is ready to praise you! I will sing and rejoice before you.

THE CHIPMUNK

The friendly little chipmunks
Give joy to those who behold
Their quick and graceful movements,
And their stripes are pretty and bold.

She is a great provider
And stores a lot of food—
With plenty for herself
And for a chipmunk brood.

He has a soft, sweet chatter—
A contented little song—
And sings for his Creator
As he hurriedly moves along.

Chipmunks are sociable little creatures and can be tamed to the point where they will eat from your hand. They are shy, but their curiosity outweighs their shyness. They are fun to watch as they dart here and there. They cache their nuts in a very convenient manner—they store them in the sleeping area and then build a bed on top. While they do not actually hibernate, they sleep much in the winter. When they are hungry, they can simply reach down to the storage area and help themselves to a snack. The chipmunk is from nine to eleven inches in length, but this includes a three-and-a-half- to four-inch tail. It is a little animal that indeed brings joy to the beholder.

Dear Lord, as the chipmunk sings its song of contentment, so my heart sings its praise to You. I too am contented . . . contented in the love and grace that You bestow on Your children, and contented in the peace that truly does pass understanding. Help me, Lord, to show my appreciation each day in the way I use the marvels You have given me.

PSALMS 66:1,2 Sing to the Lord, all the earth! Sing of his glorious name! Tell the world how wonderful he is.

THE CRICKET

Hear the cricket
Sing his song—
Sweet and peaceful,
All day long.

Fiddler, fighter,
Acrobat too—
Let him sing
His song for you.

He throws his music
From here to there—
Playing his wings
Like a fiddler rare.

He plays his tune—
He plays his song
That all creation
Might sing along.

Once you have heard a cricket chirp, you can see why so many things have been written about this homey little insect. Its chirp brings thoughts of serene summer nights and quiet days. Surely it is singing a song to its Creator. How tranquil it sounds! We can even forgive it if it nibbles our clothes as long as it keeps on singing!

Dear Lord, I love You and worship You, and, like the cricket, I will sing You a song of praise with all my heart and soul. Thank You for all of Your creations and for giving me life so that I may enjoy this beautiful world of Yours.

PSALMS 108:2–5 Wake up, O harp and lyre! We will meet the dawn with song. I will praise you everywhere around the world, in every nation. For your loving kindness is great beyond measure, high as the heavens. Your faithfulness reaches the skies. His glory is far more vast than the heavens. It towers above the earth.

THE GIBBON

Who is the smallest
In the whole ape family?
The species is the gibbon,
And he swings from tree to tree.

His legs are very long,
And his arms are longer yet.
His hands are long and slender,
And his thumbs are socket-set.

The gibbon has a "great call"—
A series of vocal sounds
That he uses at sunrise,
Or weather turnarounds.

It's a joy to watch him journey on,
Swinging from branch to branch.
He moves with such confidence,
Leaving nothing to chance.

The gibbon uses its strange call as a location signal or when sighting a troup of other gibbons. The call varies with the species. The gibbon greets a change in weather with its "great call," and also heralds the sunrise. Let us too greet the dawn with a "great call"—a cry of joy to the Lord for all He has done and continues to do for us, His children. Truly, He is everywhere—His love and kindness envelop us. He is always faithful, always true.

Dear Heavenly Father, help me to realize and appreciate all that You do for me. When I am feeling down and out, help me to praise You all the more—for I know I need to experience those bad times in order to grow. Help me to treat each day, Lord, as a learning experience—greeting each new dawn with a "great call" of thanksgiving and praise.

PSALMS 19:7–11 God's laws are perfect. They protect us, make us wise, and give us joy and light. God's laws are pure, eternal, just. They are more desirable than gold. They are sweeter than honey dripping from a honeycomb. For they warn us away from harm and give success to those who obey them.

THE HEDGEHOG

A strange creature indeed, the hedgehog,
With many, many spines.
There's a prickly and a hairy,
They hibernate—either kind.

The hedgehog is fairly small in size—
From five to twelve inches long.
His tail is short, his ears are small,
And on his feet, the claws are strong!

The spines of the hedgehog are unique—
Each is a modified hair.
He may have up to six thousand spines
To protect him from worry and care.

These little creatures are found in Asia, Africa, and Europe. They are able to roll into a ball when danger comes, protecting themselves with their spines. They are nocturnal and have a keen sense of smell and hearing. They will eat almost anything edible. They hibernate, their heart rate falling from one hundred eighty beats per minute to twenty, and the body temperature reduces greatly. Breathing almost ceases as they go into their winter sleep. The laws of nature are perfect, for they are God's laws—the laws of the Creator. How awe-inspiring they are, for they regulate all of His Creation. His laws are always for our good, and if we will follow them, He will guide and direct us to our reward in Heaven. How could one ever watch the intricate workings of nature and reject the God Who made them?

Dear Heavenly Father, truly Your laws are pure, eternal, and just. Help me to abide by the laws You provide for me, that I might be wise. I praise Your Name as Wonderful—Counselor—King of my life!

PSALMS 139:13,14 You made all the delicate, inner parts of my body, and knit them together in my mother's womb. Thank you for making me so wonderfully complex! It is amazing to think about. Your workmanship is marvelous—and how well I know it.

THE HYRAX

You can hear the hyrax calling
When the moon is shining bright.
Although they're daytime creatures,
They're also alert at night.

These little rabbitlike mammals
Grow to eighteen inches in length.
They are relatives of the elephant,
But lack the size and strength.

They are also called the "dassie"—
The "daman" or "cherogil"—
"Conies" in the Bible,
And other names as well.

Some live in rocks and some in trees—
A scientist's delight!
But they are difficult to find,
Because they hide from sight.

This little creature has been likened to the rabbit, the guinea pig, and the badger. Its bone structure in the forelegs and feet is like that of the elephant. So is its brain, and the placenta of the unborn. Its stomach and hind feet are like those of the horse, and it has a gland in the back such as the capybara of South America has on its head. It's amazing that God could use all of these similarities in one little hyrax. Still, it should not surprise us—for God created each of us, and we have such marvelously complex bodies!

Dear Lord, I bow in awe before You—Your workmanship is truly wondrous! Help me to take good care of my body—Your creation!

I JOHN 1:7 But if we are living in the light of God's presence, just as Christ does, then we have wonderful fellowship and joy with each other, and the blood of Jesus his Son cleanses us from every sin.

THE ICE FISH

An Antarctic fish with no blood
The ice fish seems to be—
And yet he must have blood to live,
This creates a quandary.

Scientists have checked this out,
And find no red cells there.
There is no hemoglobin—
This creature is quite rare!

He does have blood—but colorless,
If you can believe that!
He grows to twelve inches in length
And he is slim—not fat.

The ice fish is a slim-bodied fish. It is also called the crocodile fish because of its appearance and the shape of the head. This strange fish is an enigma to man. For many years it was believed to be actually bloodless, but around 1930, scientists found that indeed it does have blood but it lacks red cells—there is no hemoglobin, although there are a few white corpuscles. The only oxygen in the blood is a very small amount dissolved in the blood plasma. What a strange creature! We have healthy red blood, and it is often said that the life is in the blood. Our blood cleanses our body of impurities, and Jesus' blood cleanses our soul of sin. What a wonderful miracle of God! He was willing to give His life's blood as an atonement for the sins we had committed. He truly loved us—and He still does!

Dear Father in Heaven, I love You for Your great wisdom, for knowing our needs, and for filling them in such a generous way. I pray that I may emulate You, that I may give of myself to others. I thank You for the blood of Your dear Son, shed on the cross for me.

ISAIAH 66:1,2 Heaven is my throne and the earth is my footstool: What Temple can you build for me as good as that? My hand has made both earth and skies, and they are mine. Yet I will look with pity on the man who has a humble and a contrite heart, who trembles at my word.

THE JAWFISH

The jawfish live in the Virgin Isles,
In the Indo-Pacific too.
They are only four inches long,
And some have a body of blue.

The strange thing about these creatures
Is the way they build a home.
They really construct a burrow,
With several rooms to roam.

The fish line it with coral—
The construction is superb.
The end chamber is very large
So they won't be disturbed.

The jawfish gets its name from its very large mouth. It has a single dorsal fin, the front of which is supported by spiny rays. One or two of the species are mouth brooders. The remarkable thing about the jawfish is the elaborate home it builds. It may have several rooms, each lined with rocks and coral. The main chamber is quite huge for this tiny fish. How does it build such a home? The God Who created the jawfish—the God Who created man—tells us that Heaven is His throne and earth His footstool. What a great, magnificent home! He is so great that He can create worlds, and yet He loves and listens to me, if I will go to Him with a contrite heart!

Dear Lord in Heaven, everything is Yours—for You have created all. What unfathomed grace! What fathomless love! I love You and praise You, the greatest of all, for caring for a small creature like the jawfish—and me!

PSALMS 146:6,7 The God who made both earth and heaven, the seas and everything in them. He is the God who keeps every promise, and gives justice to the poor and oppressed, and food to the hungry.

THE KOALA BEAR

The gentle little koala bear
Is a loving creature.
He looks like a cuddly toy—
That's his outstanding feature.

He feeds on the eucalyptus tree;
Australia is his home.
He once was near extinction,
But now again can roam.

This happy little teddy bear
Has a little pocket
To carry "tiny teddy" in—
Nature helps to stock it.

Yes, the koala bear is a marsupial. This loveable little creature, with its leatherlike nose, clings to its mother's back long after leaving the pouch. The koala feeds solely on the eucalyptus leaves. Without this tree, it would no longer exist, but God provides its food. God also provides our food, both physically and spiritually. He has always provided His people with their needs. Praise His name for that!

Dear Lord, I praise You for Your great mercies. I thank You for providing for our physical needs. And, Lord, I thank You for our spiritual food—for Your Word. I pray that I may take full advantage of it to move ever closer to You.

PSALMS 5:3 Each morning I will look to you in heaven and lay my requests before you, praying earnestly.

THE LOON

The loon patrols his boundaries
With a plaintive call,
Sounding like a wounded child,
Echoing over all.

This bird is a fantastic diver—
Some people call him that—
And it is quite an experience
To view him in his habitat.

He will dive to fifty feet,
Looking for his prey.
His principal food is fish,
And they seldom get away!

Loons are flightless during moulting time, when they lose their wing feathers, but they are strong fliers during the rest of the year. In order to take to the air, however, they need a long runway. They patter over the water before rising to the sky. On the water, the loon often swims with the rear half of its body submerged, almost upright in the water, with neck extended and bill lifted high. This is called "plesiosaur display." Maybe we should take a cue from this and lift our eyes to the sky more often. There is no better way to start the day than with prayer. How wonderful it is to have the assurance of God's Presence throughout the day. But let's not stop there. Let us continually keep God with us, and just as the loon lifts its bill to the sky, we will lift our hearts to God.

Dear Heavenly Father, thank You for listening to my prayers and for Your answers. Help me to accept those answers, Lord, even though they are not always what I want or expect them to be. Be with me throughout every day as I turn to You for guidance.

JOHN 4:10 (Jesus) replied "If you only knew what a wonderful gift God has for you, and who I am, you would ask me for some *living water!*"

THE MOLOCH LIZARD

"Mountain devil" or "thorny devil"—
He's called either name.
The latter one describes him to a "tee."
He's like a walking thornbush
In the Northern Territory—
In Australia also, he runs free.

He is a prickly lizard,
And he has a thorny hump.
The aborigines treat him with respect.
His favorite food is tiny ants,
He eats them one by one,
And he doesn't have a tremendous intellect.

His skin surface is unique—
Different, we find.
It seems to trap the water in its grooves.
When a drop of water
Is placed upon his skin,
You can see how fast the water moves!

The moloch's total length is only six inches, and the body is round so it looks like a walking horse-chestnut burr. It is covered with thornlike spikes from head to toe. It is a slow mover, even when in a hurry; when frightened, it tucks its head between its front legs, presenting a thorny hump that stands on the back of the neck. At first it was thought that the moloch could absorb water through its skin, but now we know that the water is spread rapidly through minute grooves. If you dip the tail in water, the entire skin surface will be wet within seconds. The small creature makes use of every drop. We have access to the Living Water that Jesus spoke of. Let us partake of it fully and completely—every day of our lives.

Dear Heavenly Father, I thank You for providing for me . . . for standing by me no matter what I do . . . and for helping me to learn from life's experiences. I pray that I may be immersed in the Living Water of Your Word and filled with the Spirit of Your love.

PSALMS 33:1 Let all the joys of the godly well up in praise to the Lord, for it is right to praise him.

THE NIGHTINGALE

A nightingale singing
On a moonlit night
Will make your heart
Leap with delight.

The bird itself
Is small and plain,
But the song he sings
Is a joyful refrain.

He sings at night
When all is still,
And captures your heart
With his happy trill.

This little bird, so often an inspiration for poetry and prose, is quite unimpressive to look at. Male and female are alike—about six and a half inches long with russet feathers above, dull white below, and a bright, rufous tail and rump. It is a shy bird and seldom seen. It prefers to hide in the undergrowth. It is a ground feeder. The chicks are speckled, and there may be up to five of them, once a year. Why does the nightingale sing at night? Ornithologists have come up with the view that it sings for the sheer joy of living. We too can let our joy show in our praise to God. It does not have to be at a certain place or at a certain time—as long as it is constantly welling up from our hearts and spilling out to those around us.

Dear Father in Heaven, let me—like the nightingale—sing a song of praise and joy that I have You and this wonderful world that You created. Praise be to You for Your Son, Who died on the cross that I might have eternal life.

GALATIANS 6:14 As for me, God forbid that I should boast about anything except the cross of our Lord Jesus Christ.

THE ORB SPIDER

A cartwheel web
The orb spider weaves—
A beautiful trap
That often deceives.

He must depend
On his web for prey
To give him nourishment
Day after day.

And so he weaves
A web in the sun—
A work of art
When it is done.

A work of art—
A victim's end,
The balance of nature
Must defend.

The orb spider has a large body for its size. The half-inch body may vary from pale fawn to rich brown. The male is smaller than the female. The webs spun by the spider are so strong and large that they have been used as fishing nets in parts of Southeast Asia. The local people bend a pliable stick into a loop at the end and weave it through the web. This little creature carries a very distinctive pattern on its abdomen—a group of five white spots that form a perfect cross. All of Creation is woven into God's plan for us, and we are reminded of this over and over again in nature. We have nothing to boast about but that cross—the cross of our Lord, Jesus Christ.

Dear Heavenly Father, I love You and praise You for all Your blessings! Help me to remember the great sacrifice that was made on the cross of Calvary, and I pray that I may live as You would want me to.

PSALMS 5:11,12 But make everyone rejoice who puts his trust in you. Keep them shouting for joy because you are defending them. Fill all who love you with your happiness. For you bless the godly man, O Lord; you protect him with your shield of love.

THE PALM DOVE

These pretty birds,
With their bubbling laughter,
Leave an echo of joy
Lingering after.

They're small and dainty,
With softly hued colors,
Only half the size
Of most of the others.

When people hear them
As they bill and coo,
They're thought to say,
"Darling, I love you."

Isn't the love of God wonderful? This beautiful little bird seems to shout it out. The head, neck, and breast are pink-tinged, the abdomen white. The back is chestnut-colored, and the rump is slate blue. The tail is brown, edged with gray and white. There is a colorful bib around the neck. These sweet songsters are also known as town, village, or garden doves. They are easily tamed, and they are seed eaters. Their main call is four to six "coos" together, which give the effect of a bubbling, happy laugh—a very attractive sound. It is a popular bird for all of these reasons. It brings joy to those around it, and we also should bring joy to those around us. We have the greatest cause of joy there can ever be! Christ, the Son of God! Praise the Lord!

Dear Heavenly Father, I thank You for giving us such joy and the freedom to share it with others. I pray that all people may receive that happy gift with open hearts and open hands.

PSALMS 9:1,2 O Lord, I will praise you with all my heart, and tell everyone about the marvelous things you do. I will be glad, yes, filled with joy because of you. I will sing your praises, O Lord God above all gods.

THE PEACOCK

The peacock's very beauty,
With his open fan,
Gives a living testimony
Of Creation unto man.

You can't behold this marvel
Without a joyful heart.
He sings out in living color
Of God's love from the start.

The beauty of the peacock
Is just a little taste
Of the wondrous sight of Heaven—
Of the beauty of His grace!

The peacock starts out in life as a drab brown, but, oh, the coat that is in store for it! It takes two years for the train, or "nautch," to develop, but by then it may be from forty to fifty inches long. With the tail, this can be a magnificent six feet in length. The beautiful feathers are shed in the late summer and grow back by the end of the year. The primary work of the peacock seems to be that of adding beauty to this old world, and it certainly does a good job of it. The peacock shouts of the Glory of God by its very appearance. Let us also praise God by our lives—by the beauty of our spirit and the thoughtfulness of our actions. We are always a witness, either for or against God.

Dear Lord, I pray that my witness may always be for You. I pray that I may wear the colors of purity, truth, and love. I praise You for giving us this gorgeous creature, the peacock, as a reminder of the beauty of Creation.

PSALMS 147:1 Hallelujah! Yes, praise the Lord! How good it is to sing his praises! How delightful, and how right!

THE SCRUBBIRD

The noisy little scrubbird
Belongs to a species rare!
He lives in far Australia,
And the number is small there.

He nests in the eucalypt forest,
Down in the densest part,
And though his song is noisy,
It comes right from the heart.

His melody rings sweetly—
Unafraid and clear—
Let us sing as strongly,
That others may also hear!

People are always amazed at how loudly the scrubbird sings. Loud and true! It is a poor flier and spends most of its time running rapidly through the scrub. It is capable of short flights up to six feet from the ground. The species measures from six and a half to eight and three-quarters inches long. It eats insects, and as it runs along the ground searching for food, it looks much like a little mouse. One egg is laid at a time, and the female takes care of the egg and the young chick. As the little scrubbird sings its song loud and clear, shouldn't we? We have the most precious song of all to share—the song of salvation. Let us sing out our joy in the Lord that others may hear and join us in our song!

Dear Lord, give me the courage to "sing out" for You. I pray that I might not be shy about sharing the message of eternal life. Help me to sing out loud and clear—like the scrubbird— through the way I live and through the way I conduct myself in my dealings with others.

HEBREWS 4:14 But Jesus the Son of God is our great High Priest who has gone to heaven itself to help us; therefore let us never stop trusting him.

THE SURICATE

The suricate, a mongoose,
Loves the bright sunlight.
He'll stand in it to sunbathe
When the weather's right.

He's a friendly creature,
And lives in colonies.
He's good at catching rats and snakes
And mice in quantities.

He isn't very pretty,
And the smallest of his kind.
His home is in South Africa,
Enjoying the sunshine.

This creature looks like an odd mixture of dog, starving raccoon, and lemur. It is ten to fourteen inches in height with about an eight-inch tail. Its coat is soft gray with a reddish undercoat. Its head is almost white, and its back carries black stripes across it. The ears are black, as is the tip of the tail. It is quite slender in build. The suricate is a real "sun-worshiper" and is most often seen basking in the sunlight, either laying down or sitting on its haunches facing the sun. We too should be "Son-worshipers," with our eyes always on Christ. As the sun gives the suricate the warmth it craves, so the Lord provides us with the warmth of His love. As we are filled with the radiance of the Spirit, it will radiate out to others. As we become more like Him, we will be a living witness to the Son.

Dear Lord, I pray that I may be filled with the Son's rays in the form of Your Holy Spirit—that I may radiate Your love to others so they may see You within me.

PSALMS 95:6,7 Come, kneel before the Lord our Maker, for he is our God. We are his sheep and he is our Shepherd. Oh, that you would hear him calling you today and come to him!

THE WARTHOG

Africa is the continent
Of the warthog family.
They like to wallow in the mud,
And just graze quietly.

The male is unaggressive,
But if danger should arise,
He'd be quite able to defend
His mate and piglet prize.

They prefer the open country,
And love the tender weed,
Although they often drop to their knees
In order to reach—to feed.

The warthog is quite ugly, having large wartlike projections on the face. Its head is very long, and it has tusks. The tusks can be a foot or more in length and are used for digging or for defense. Indeed, they can inflict a serious wound! These creatures have very short necks and often find it necessary to drop to their padded knees to feed. Let us kneel too as we contemplate God's tender mercies. Sometimes we need to take the time to just be still and know that He is God. He is our Shepherd, and we are the sheep of His pasture. I cannot think of a better place to be.

Dear Heavenly Father, I kneel in adoration before You. I cannot imagine how life would be without You—You are my friend, my confidant, my Savior, my God! When it comes right down to it, Lord, all I am or ever will be are wrapped up in You. Without You, I would be nothing. With You beside me and within me, I can be anything and do anything I strive for, in Your will.

5
Perseverance

ECCLESIASTES 7:14 Enjoy prosperity whenever you can, and when hard times strike, realize that God gives one as well as the other—so that everyone will realize that nothing is certain in this life.

THE ALBATROSS

The hardy bird called the albatross
Lives upon the sea.
His food is fish and floating squid
He catches carefully.

He soars high above the ocean,
Or rides upon the waves—
He's silent and stoic in flight
As the storms and winds he braves.

It lays one egg, quite large in size,
And the parents both incubate.
The chick emerges in two months—
Sometimes it may be late!

The albatross nests on high island cliffs, and that downy little chick takes from four to nine months to become a fledgling. In the largest species, the albatross may reach a twelve-foot wing span. Its toes are webbed, and it swims well on the water's surface, although it is really not equipped for diving. What a sight to see a number of them soaring and gliding around a ship! They never seem to complain, but when a storm comes, they silently weather it out. They are very seldom seen on land. The albatross seems to take what comes with calm aplomb. Frequently we too must weather through. God never promised us an easy pathway, but He *did* promise to walk beside us. Therefore, no matter what may come, we can rejoice in our Lord. Blue skies always follow the storm, and smiles will wipe away the tears.

Dear Heavenly Father, I thank You for the good times and the bad. Help me to realize that just as the storm clears the atmosphere, so the bad times can be used to my betterment. Help me to use my trials to grow in my Christian walk. I praise You, Lord, for being so wise and all-knowing—and for helping me to weather the storms of life.

GALATIANS 6:4,5 Let everyone be sure that he is doing his very best, for then he will have the personal satisfaction of work well done, and won't need to compare himself with someone else. Each of us must bear some faults and burdens of his own. For none of us is perfect!

THE ARROW-POISON FROG

Though such a little creature—
And this frog is really small—
Of all of God's creations,
He's the deadliest of all.

One little kokoi frog,
Just an inch in length,
Can poison fifty arrows—
Lethal in their strength.

The female lays the eggs—
The male takes them in.
He carries them on his back,
Attached to his skin.

These tiny creatures are truly deadly! Most arrow-poison frogs can be distinguished by the naillike plate on each toe. Many are brightly colored. They are found only in Central and South America, where the Indians use the venom on arrowheads. The female lays the eggs on the ground and then the male fertilizes them, after which it carries the eggs on its back (how they get there is a mystery), and they become attached to its skin. After hatching, the tadpoles remain on their father's back, getting moisture from the rain. Up to twenty tadpoles may be found on a single male. When they are big enough, the father goes down to the water and the young swim off on their own. How often do we feel dependent, like the little tadpoles, and expect others to handle our problems for us? We have God's protection and the Holy Spirit's guidance—what more do we need? Our friends may be happy to give us encouragement and a listening ear—but, in the long run, we must each handle our own responsibilities.

Dear Lord, thank You for dear friends. I pray that I may be responsible enough and loving enough to refrain from imposing my problems on them. I thank You for the Holy Spirit and for the strength and encouragement You provide.

JOHN 7:37b,38 If anyone is thirsty, let him come to me and drink. For the Scriptures declare that rivers of living water shall flow from the inmost being of anyone who believes in me.

THE CAMEL

This oddity of the desert
Has one hump or two.
The camel's fat is concentrated
In the humps we view.

Camels carry their own water,
And do not dehydrate.
They control their body temperature,
And the heat can tolerate.

They are sturdy creatures,
And travel very well.
They can run for sixty miles,
And you can hardly tell.

Actually, the camel has been known to cover a hundred miles in a day. It can go for ten days without water, traveling sixty or seventy miles a day. Just as the camel carries its water supply for strength and endurance, so do we. In the Book of John, Jesus speaks of the Living Water that He provides. When we accept Him as Savior, we are provided with this great source of power—and, indeed, it gives us the strength and endurance we need for our journey through this earthly life. In its journeys, a camel rarely stumbles or falls. We may stumble—and even fall—but, praise God, He is always there to lift us up and start us on our way again.

Dear Lord, I thank You for the Living Water You provide. You have given me so many blessings—I pray that I may live my life to the fullest for You, using well all the gifts You have so generously bestowed.

COLOSSIANS 1:11,12 We are praying, too, that you will be filled with his mighty, glorious strength so that you can keep going no matter what happens—always full of the joy of the Lord, and always thankful to the Father who has made us fit to share all the wonderful things that belong to those who live in the kingdom of light.

THE CHAMELEON

The lizard we call "chameleon"
Lives in shrubs and trees.
His feet are made like clasping tongs—
He holds to his perch with ease.

His tongue is long and sticky
So he can catch his prey—
His eyes work independently,
But he can see okay.

He can change his color
And almost disappear.
He matches his environment
When danger comes too near.

There are ninety chameleon species, ranging from a few centimeters in length to a reported thirty-two inches. The chameleon is found primarily in tropical Africa and Madagascar. Its tongue can be shot out to a length even greater than its body, so it has no trouble in catching prey. The tongue is clublike on the end, and sticky. The chameleon changes color to blend with its surroundings during the day. However, when the little creatures let down their defenses in sleep, most of them fade to a pale whitish color and are easy to capture by torchlight. We too are easy prey if we let our relationship with God "sleep." Let us always be full of the joy and peace that Christ offers us. Let us "keep on keeping on," no matter what the circumstances, always praising Him and relying on His help and comfort.

Dear Heavenly Father, I pray that I may always be full of the joy You offer, and please help me to share it with those around me. I pray that You will fill me with Your Spirit, and I thank You for letting me live in Your Kingdom of Light.

HEBREWS 10:36 You need to keep on patiently doing God's will if you want him to do for you all that he has promised.

THE CHIMPANZEE

They're smart little apes, the chimpanzees—
It's amazing what they can do.
They're adept at using objects as tools,
And know when to use them too.

They'll use a stick to extract food
Or to drive a foe away,
And they'll use leaves to make a sponge
For drinking or water-play.

They can run upon the ground,
Or swing from branch to branch.
They are very sociable,
And visit at every chance.

They build a nest wherever they are—
They follow no permanent plan.
They feed on fruit, leaves, nuts, and bark—
Ants and termites too, when they can.

The chimpanzee is one of two African apes, a brother to the larger gorilla. Adults may weigh up to one hundred and ten pounds. The flesh-colored skin of the infant turns to black in the adult. They are very intelligent and make use of natural objects for their own purposes. They will poke a stick into a nest of wild bees and bring it out dripping with succulent honey, or into a hill of termites and wait until the stick is covered with the dainty morsels. They must be patient, and the promise of a good meal is their reward. But our reward for patience is so much greater! If we live our lives in God's will, doing as He would have us do for the furtherance of His Kingdom, our patience and endurance will bring us the reward of eternal life in Heaven!

Dear Heavenly Father, help me to patiently perform the tasks You set before me. Help me to be patient with others and myself, that I might grow in wisdom and understanding.

PSALMS 55:6–8 Oh, for wings like a dove, to fly away and rest! I would fly to the far off deserts and stay there. I would flee to some refuge from all this storm.

THE DOVE

The dove is a pretty bird to see.
His cooing sound is sweet.
He comes in many colors,
And he likes seeds to eat.

Most species are gregarious,
And can be seen in flocks.
They adapt to their environment,
Both the hens and cocks.

Their wings are strong and sturdy too—
This bird is not afraid.
Many live in cities,
By people undismayed.

The dove and the pigeon have no biological distinction. With their strong wings, they can fly away, as David in the Book of Psalms longed to. Instead, many species have learned to live with man and his civilization and survive. They have adapted to their environment and, for the most part, thrive in it. We too must learn to adapt to less-than-perfect conditions—to make the most of what we have and to do the best we can in the circumstances in which we find ourselves. Sometimes it would be so nice to fly away from our problems, but— like the dove—we must learn to cope.

Dear Lord, please help me today to face my problems head-on and solve them with Your counsel instead of trying to blot them out or run away from them. I know that there is no victory without a battle, and so I pray that I may be victorious for You in the face of every challenge I meet.

MATTHEW 5:15,16 Don't hide your light! Let it shine for all; let your good deeds glow for all to see, so that they will praise your heavenly Father.

THE FIREFLY

Have you seen a firefly
Upon a hot summer's night?
From the quiet darkness
Comes a blinking signal-light.

This brave little blinker
Is not the fly he seems to be.
He really is a member
Of the beetle family.

His light is not to guide him,
For it glows from his back end—
It's not for his protection,
For it shows where he has been.

But he keeps his love-light shining,
And it casts its glow afar,
Blinking through the darkness
Like a tiny twinkling star.

There are several species of fireflies. Some of them are quite small, and some that inhabit the tropics are quite large and bright. Their light is an enigma to us, although we are coming closer to the secret of this cool, heatless illumination. It seems to act as a signal between the sexes, and the periodic flashes are perfectly timed. Just as the firefly lights his own little corner of the world, so should we. If each of us would hold his light high, we could chase away the darkness of sin. One candle does not give much light, true—but fill a room with twinkling tapers and watch the darkness disappear! Let our lights so shine!

Dear Father in Heaven, I thank You for the opportunity to carry the Light for You. I pray that I may run this race of life without dropping or blowing out that Light, which is generated by Christ Jesus.

PROVERBS 3:21–23 Have two goals: wisdom—that is, knowing and doing right—and common sense. Don't let them slip away, for they fill you with living energy, and are a feather in your cap. They keep you safe from defeat and disaster and from stumbling off the trail.

THE FOX

Red fox, silver fox,
Black or gray—
An animal as intelligent
As any are today.

The fox is sly and wily,
He's bold as he can be—
He's actually a help to man,
If allowed to remain free.

He feeds on carrion and mice,
And will not bother men
Unless driven by hunger,
When he may kill a hen.

The fox uses all of its intelligence and cunning in everything it does. It needs all of its wiles because it is so widely hunted for its fur. Men the world over hunt this small animal, and he is never really safe. In the same way that the fox has enemies who pursue it constantly, so do we. Our predators are Satan and this world of his. He can actually make sin look attractive—he baits his traps so well. We must use all of our wisdom and common sense to escape our enemies and follow Christ's Way.

Dear Lord, help me to be constantly on guard against my enemy, the devil. Teach me to use all my intelligence and wisdom for the furtherance of Your Kingdom here on earth and in Heaven. Guide me and direct me as I grow in my Christian walk.

PROVERBS 20:27 A man's conscience is the Lord's searchlight exposing his hidden motives.

THE HONEY GUIDE

*These birds often lay their eggs
In someone else's home.
The eggs are hatched by other birds,
Who treat them like their own.*

*Honey guides have the ability
to smell out honeybees.
They'll lead a man or badger
To a beehive in the trees.*

*When the honeycomb is broken,
They use their short, stout bills.
Their thick skin protects from stings,
And the honey guides eat their fill!*

This strange little bird does not even hatch its own eggs. It finds someone else to do the job for it. It also finds someone else to break open the beehive so it can feast. It will lead a honey badger or a man to the hive, calling and cajoling all the way. The honey guide is only doing what nature intends it to do. We also must do what God intended us to do. Truly, the conscience within each of us—lit by the Light of the Holy Spirit—makes clear His intentions and what our actions should be. Let us strive to make sure they are one and the same!

Dear Heavenly Father, let me live by Your laws, just as the honey guide lives by the laws You have set for it. I fail so many times Lord, but I pray You will be patient with me as I keep on trying.

JOHN 4:34 Then Jesus explained: "My nourishment comes from doing the will of God who sent me, and from finishing his work."

THE KIWI BIRD

The strange-looking kiwi bird
Is hardly a bird at all.
He lives in the "bush" in New Zealand,
And is fifteen inches tall.

His body is covered with feathers
That resemble shaggy brown hair.
He's a ground bird, the strange kiwi,
And never flies in the air.

Stranger still, the kiwi egg
Is large and slow to hatch.
The chick emerges hungry,
And immediately starts to scratch!

The kiwi is a nocturnal bird, hiding in the daytime and foraging for food at night. It grows very slowly and takes from three to five years to mature, even though the egg is large and the bird emerges with a coat of feathers. The kiwi is not equipped to fly, but it does very well on the ground. It feeds on worms, digging deep in the earth with its long beak. It also eats insects, berries, and beetle larvae. In the Scripture above, Jesus was speaking to the woman of Samaria at the well. Because we are God's children, our nourishment is provided by the same Source that nourished our Savior. As the kiwi digs deep into the earth for its energy supply, so do we dig deep into God's Word for ours, that we might know His will in our lives.

Dear Father in Heaven, I pray that I might be in the center of Your will, daily nourished by Your Word. Help me to listen, Lord, when You speak and to do what You would have me do in this short span of life on earth.

PSALMS 30:4,5 Oh, sing to him you saints of his; give thanks to his holy name. His anger lasts a moment; his favor lasts for life! Weeping may go on all night, but in the morning there is joy.

THE LEATHERY TURTLE

Late at night, four times a year,
The leathery turtle comes ashore.
This rare creature of the sea
Opens imagination's door.

She comes on land to lay her eggs,
Then she's out to sea again.
Some turtles can be enormous
And have often startled men.

The shells they carry on their backs
Are made up of many strong plates.
These turtles have extra-oily skin,
And are really heavyweights!

The leathery turtles do not carry barnacles and seaweed on their shells as other turtles do. This is probably because of their extra-oily skin. They are fast swimmers despite the fact that they may weigh up to eight hundred pounds. This big turtle is known to cry mightily when it comes ashore. Why? It may be to remove sand from its eyes or to get rid of excess salt from the seawater. We do not really know the reason for the turtle's tears. How then can we really know the reason for human tears? We may shed tears because of sorrow or pain. Even Jesus wept at Lazarus' death. There are many occasions for tears in this old world. We are told in Scripture that there will be no cause for tears in Heaven. Praise the Lord, He has promised us a bright and beautiful future!

Dear Heavenly Father, we thank You for the bright future ahead. Whatever this world may bring, we know that someday we will be rejoicing with You on Heaven's shores. Praise Your Holy Name!

PROVERBS 28:1 The wicked flee when no one is chasing them! But the godly are bold as lions!

THE LION

The lion, king of Africa,
Really has it made.
The females do the hunting,
While the male rests in the shade.

This mighty macho figure
Is an emblem of the bold,
And whether up or resting,
He's a marvel to behold.

He looks quite impressive
With his wondrous flowing mane.
It is his crown of glory
In his kingdom on the plain.

Master of his universe,
When he gives a roar,
The great and mighty lion
Gets what he's looking for!

This great, impressive-looking cat has built quite a reputation for itself. We know that the females do the hunting and that they must be good at it in order to feed the "pride," as the group is called. The lion is a bold and beautiful animal, afraid of virtually nothing. It proudly upholds its reputation as king of beasts. We should try to be like the lion, proudly holding up the name of Christ that others might know Him for what He is—the King of Glory.

Dear Father in Heaven, I pray that I may hold Your banner high and serve as a bold and fearless witness of my Lord and Savior. Help me to be filled with Your Holy Spirit and to persevere in my efforts to win more souls for You.

GALATIANS 6:9 And let us not get tired of doing what is right, for after a while we will reap a harvest of blessing if we don't get discouraged and give up.

THE MOCKINGBIRD

The mockingbird has a lovely voice
And a repertoire of song.
He listens to another bird,
And then he sings along.

There is a legend that's been told
That the first song he trills
Is submission unto God—
It means "If God wills."

The male bird does the singing
And while the female nests,
He watches from a vantage point
And sings his very best.

While the eggs are hatching out—
From dawn 'til darkest night,
He sits there guarding his family,
And sings with all his might.

Until the chicks can leave the nest,
We hear the singer trill—
He'll dive-bomb any enemies
With his pointed bill.

The mockingbird is second only to the hermit thrush in the beauty of its voice. And, incredibly, the mockingbird has been known to mimic the songs of forty different birds. It has amazing stamina as it watches over the nest—singing all the while. The song that says, "The mockingbird is singing all the day," is certainly truthful. We too should "sing all the day," never tiring of serving our Father. As the mockingbird waits for the "harvest," its young family, so we can look forward to harvesting our reward of life eternal with God.

Dear Heavenly Father, I thank You for Your many blessings. Help me to "keep on keeping on," not becoming discouraged and falling by the way but continually singing Your song. Should I stumble, Lord, help me to grasp the hand You hold out to me and—sturdy again on my feet—continue my Christian journey for You.

HEBREWS 3:14 For if we are faithful to the end, trusting God just as we did when we first became Christians, we will share in all that belongs to Christ.

THE MUDSKIPPER

In the mangrove swamps
Lives a creature small and strange.
He's classified a fish,
But he's increased his range.

When the tide goes out
And leaves a murky, muddy mess,
He does not expire,
But puts forth his very best.

He breathes the newfound air
As he moves over the mud.
This fish is a real survivor,
In famine or in flood!

The mudskipper is tadpole-like, from five to twelve inches long. It is equipped to live in the water or out. It is found in Africa and the Indo-Australian region. It lives its life from day to day—whatever comes, it makes the best of it. Can we do less? As Christians, we must keep on faithfully living for the Lord, whatever comes our way. If sometimes you feel like a "fish out of water," just think of the mudskipper and continue on with your life.

Dear Heavenly Father, help me take a lesson from the odd little mudskipper and keep on going when conditions are bad. Help me to realize that whatever may come, You will provide for me. I look on the future with anticipation, knowing that I will eventually be with You in Your perfect home!

II SAMUEL 22:36 You have given me the shield of your salvation; your gentleness has made me great.

THE OCEAN SUNFISH

Shaped like a millstone
And weighing a ton,
These strange creatures
Got their name from the sun.

When they were seen on the surface,
The story was so told,
They came up to sunbathe—
To get out of the cold.

Now we are wiser—
We know they surface when ill.
When they are healthy,
They swim where they will!

The ocean sunfish may swim near the surface or it may go down to six-hundred-foot depths. It usually travels singly or with one other. The spinal cord is only half an inch long, and the brain is very small. Its body is oval and covered with a thick, leathery skin—gray, brown, or black—with silver highlights. The largest of the species may weigh a ton and be ten feet long. It is very slow, and instead of trying to escape a predator (including man), it holds its ground and grunts and groans. These sounds are made by grinding its throat teeth. It does not bother to try to get away because it has a two- to three-inch coat of gristle under the tough skin. Even a bullet will not penetrate. Just as this tough coating acts as a shield against predators, so does our "shield of salvation" from God protect us from the devil. Because of God's love and mercy, we need have no fear of our enemies.

Dear Lord in Heaven, help me to be more and more like You—evergrowing in gentleness and love. Help me to have empathy for others and to remember to hold up my shield of salvation with pride and praise for You.

II CORINTHIANS 4:17,18 These troubles and sufferings of ours are, after all, quite small and won't last very long. Yet this short time of distress will result in God's richest blessing upon us forever and ever! So we do not look at what we can see right now, the troubles all around us, but we look forward to the joys in heaven which we have not yet seen. The troubles will soon be over, but the joys to come will last forever.

THE OYSTER

The oyster is a mollusk
With a double shell.
When it comes to eating,
The oyster does quite well.

Water passes through it,
Bringing the oyster food.
If the water's turbid,
Impurities may intrude.

But that smart old oyster
Coats them with a swirl,
Until that grain of trouble
Turns into a pearl!

The oyster is a primitive bivalve, famed as food. It has a system of filtration that works very well in clear water. Occasionally, however, a small grain of sand or some other obstruction will get caught inside the shell. The oyster simply coats it over and over again, thus creating a pearl from a problem. Sometimes we have trouble in facing our problems. But God uses the principle of the pearl for us too. The troubles we face today are the very obstructions that will be used by Him to perfect us for His Kingdom.

Dear Lord, help me to use Your pearl principle. The next time something irritates me, help me to coat it with love and understanding, thereby creating my own pearl from a problem. Help me to smooth the rough edges in my life, Lord, that I might be worthy of Your Kingdom.

EPHESIANS 5:19 Talk with each other much about the Lord, quoting psalms and hymns and singing sacred songs, making music in your hearts to the Lord.

THE PENGUIN

Penguins love society,
And seldom live alone.
Their colonies can be quite huge
In all the species known.

They prefer the Southern Hemisphere
And spend much time in the sea.
They hunt while in the water,
Swimming expertly.

They look very debonair,
Dressed in black and white.
Out of the water, with their webbed feet,
They walk like a man—upright.

The penguin varies from almost four feet in height to one foot, according to the species. Most penguins are the traditional black and white with the exception of the Emperor (the largest), which has a pale yellow chest and abdomen. They are excellent swimmers and walk upright on their webbed feet when out of the water. However, when they are in a hurry, they slide on their abdomens on the ice and snow! Penguin colonies may number several million; they are indeed social creatures, and very vocal about it too. They build their nests close together and chatter incessantly. We are social beings also, and it is very important that we spend time with our fellow Christians in praising God in unison. We need this constant contact with one another to keep us strong in our faith and in our love and regard for our Father.

Dear Lord, help me to "fill up" on Christian fellowship so I may joyously deal with the workaday world, cherishing my brothers and sisters in Your Name. Thank You for providing me with the "family of God."

I THESSALONIANS 4:11,12a This should be your ambition: to live a quiet life, minding your own business and doing your own work, just as we told you before. As a result, people who are not Christians will trust and respect you.

THE RABBIT

Have you seen a jack rabbit
Or a cottontail
Running through the bright meadow?
It seems that they can sail!

They seem so very ordinary
When you take a glance,
But when you really study them,
You find they're quite advanced.

They play such complicated games,
And though they may be small,
They are very important
In the blueprint of it all.

They change coats in wintertime,
From brown or gray to white.
They blend in with the scenery,
And are protected day and night.

The mighty rabbits, small in size,
Are quiet and serene,
And yet they have a big impact
On Mother Nature's scene.

The wild rabbit goes its way—living its life in an unobtrusive manner—and yet what an impact it has on nature! It is a "basic food animal," which means that if there are a lot of rabbits, everything else multiplies too. The wolves leave the deer alone—the deer feed on the grasses, which allows new grasses to grow, and so forth. The nature cycle continues. Yes, the quiet, unobtrusive rabbit is really a very important cog in the wheel of nature. So should we be—living our lives in harmony and showing the world by example what Christ can do.

Dearest Lord Jesus, help me to realize that it is not always the grand and glorious acts that count, but the everyday living for You. It is the little things that mount up that matter. Help me to have the will to continue my Christian climb, steadily, quietly, and with determination.

PSALMS 5:8 Lord, lead me as you promised me you would . . . tell me clearly what to do, which way to turn.

THE SALMON

The feisty little salmon,
Born in a riverbed,
Heads out to the open sea
As though he's being led.

After years of growing,
His instinct takes him back—
Back to where he started from
In his fish egg sac.

His strong and silvery body
Is bruised and weaker grows
As he jumps the rocks and falls,
And fights the reverse flows.

He knows he must accomplish
One thing before he dies—
He must reach his birthplace
And new eggs fertilize.

Yes, the salmon, if it is lucky enough to escape its many foes—porpoises, seals, lampreys, and man, to name a few—always returns to its birthplace to renew the life cycle. Pacific salmon die after reproduction, but the Atlantic salmon sometimes manages to get back to the sea, and the process repeats itself. The instinct of the salmon guides it in its journeys just as the Holy Spirit guides us, if we will take the time to listen. Sometimes it seems that we, as Christians, are "bucking the current" too, but if we exercise endurance in this journey of life, we will win the prize. As the salmon lays its eggs and renews the life cycle, so do we renew our life with Christ through our prayers for His guidance.

Dear Lord, give me the obedience and endurance that the salmon demonstrates. Help me to keep my eyes ever on You so that the currents of the worldly elements that swirl around me can never dim the sound of Your Voice.

JAMES 1:14–16 Temptation is the pull of man's own evil thoughts and wishes. These evil thoughts lead to evil actions and afterwards to the death penalty from God. So don't be misled, dear brothers.

THE SEA ANEMONE

There never was a stranger sight
Than a living anemone.
He comes in many colors,
This "flower of the sea."

"Anemone" is Greek for "wind,"
And he is found worldwide.
His home is always in the sea,
And he may move with the tide.

His tentacles will paralyze
As they surround his prey.
He's a voracious eater,
And will eat any time of day.

He will survive, however,
Without any food to eat,
And even though he shrinks in size,
Just surviving is a feat!

The sea anemone is a beautiful sight. It comes as a shock, then, to see it consume its prey! Those beautiful, floating tentacles, so delicate, seem to beckon to the victim, enticing it to come within reach. Then they wrap around the unwary prey, paralyzing it with the poison they exude as they carry it to the mouth. Just as those tentacles beckon to the prey, so temptation often beckons to us. We must be on our guard and realize that temptation is never from God but from the devil working through self. The end is the same as the anemone's prey—death. Temptation will either make us stronger by exercising our resistance or weaker should we give in to it.

Dear Heavenly Father, help me to remember that without a battle, no victory is won. Give me strength to meet the foe. Help me to fight temptation with the Spirit, for I know that I cannot win alone. Strengthen me that I might daily grow stronger in Christ Jesus.

ROMANS 8:38,39 For I am convinced that nothing can ever separate us from his love. Death can't, and life can't. The angels won't, and all the powers of hell itself cannot keep God's love away. Our fears for today, our worries about tomorrow, or where we are—high above the sky, or in the deepest ocean—nothing will ever be able to separate us from the love of God demonstrated by our Lord Jesus Christ when he died for us.

THE SNAIL

Flamingo Tongue, the Garden Snail,
And Periwinkle too—
The Cowrie and the Purple Sea,
In shells of different hue.

They slowly creep along their way,
Oiling the path they take—
Undaunted by the obstacles
That otherwise might break.

They carry their houses upon their backs
And never cease to be
A great source of amazement
To humans such as me.

It takes an ordinary snail all of one minute to travel a distance of three inches. As it moves, it pours out a fluid to coat the path in front of it. Thus the alien fluids and dust in the way are covered and will not affect the little creature's course. The old adage, "slow as a snail," may have a basis in fact, but although the snail is slow, it is consistent. No matter what obstacle may be in the way, it continues on its journey at the same pace, arriving at its destination as fresh and clean as when it left the starting point. Nothing can deter it from its course. Just as the snail coats its path and slowly and consistently follows it, so God coats our path with His grace and love as we follow Him. No matter what the obstacles, He is with us, and nothing can part us but we ourselves. It is only when we cease to follow that we lose our way.

Dear Lord, thank You for the guidance You extend. Give me the patience and courage to follow the path You lay out for me. Help me to overcome the obstacles in my Christian walk. I praise Your Holy Name for the mercy and grace You bestow on me.

PSALMS 107:28–30 Then they cry to the Lord in their trouble, and he saves them. He calms the storm and stills the waves. What a blessing is that stillness, as he brings them safely into harbor!

THE STORM PETREL

The storm petrel may be small,
But he rides out a storm,
Hugging the surface of the waves
On the air currents that form.

Petrels are often seen at sea,
Flitting in the wake of ships—
Feeding on small crustaceans
Brought up by the waves and dips.

They appear to walk upon
The water as they feed.
Wings outstretched and legs straight down,
They look strange indeed!

These little birds, only five to ten inches long, brave the high seas in their quest for food. There are twenty known species, and they belong to the same family as the albatross, but they are—oh, so much smaller! The storm petrel is often called the "Jesus bird" because of the way it appears to walk on the water. Another name used is "Mother Carey's chicken," probably after the Virgin Mary (Mater Cara). The storm petrel can ride out a storm very well unless the wind changes. Then it is left without any help from the air currents and must try to manage alone. Isn't that the truth with us too! We can manage the storms of life as long as the Lord is with us to calm the sea, but when we take off on our own, we usually end up in trouble. We need Jesus at the helm!

Dear Lord, please take the helm of my life in Your hands and teach me to stop trying to do things my way. I know from past experience that it only gets me in trouble. I need You to calm the seas and guide me through. Praise You for always being there!

6
Self-Control

PROVERBS 20:11 The character of even a child can be known by the way he acts—whether what he does is pure and right.

THE ALLIGATOR

Beware the alligator
As he suns upon the bank.
You may think he's smiling,
But he is sure a crank!

He looks quite slow and clumsy,
Yet he may take you by surprise.
He uses lightning speed
When something takes his eye.

His jaws and teeth are deadly—
He can snap a log in two.
His temper, too, is surly.
What harm he can do!

Would you believe that baby alligators are born as cantankerous as their elders? About ten inches long, they charge out of that egg all ready for a fight. Indeed, their character is known by the way they act! So it is with us. No matter how we may try to disguise it, our true character will show through our actions. Let us just make sure that what shows is pure and right.

Dear Heavenly Father, I pray that my character might take on the attributes of Jesus Christ. I hope that as I mature physically, I might also mature spiritually and that I might be a good witness for You.

PROVERBS 17:14 It is hard to stop a quarrel once it starts, so don't let it begin.

THE BABOON

Baboons, homely though they be,
Teach a lesson to you and me.
They live in groups, and socialize;
In their own way, they're very wise.
But one thing seems to be so true—
In studying them, I share with you,
They are a wonder to perceive,
And would you listen and believe
They live in harmony until
One starts a fight—one usually will—
And when a fight is once begun,
It strikes a spark in every one,
And soon a chain reaction starts,
And many fights drive them apart.
Now have you known a human being
That acts like this? Yes, have you seen
A troublemaker who enjoys
Causing problems to annoy?
Let us pray that we will be
Peaceful and live in harmony!

The Lord promises us, as Christians, the peace that passes all understanding. Why then, with this promise, do we still allow disharmony with our brothers and sisters in the Lord? We say, "It's only human nature!" True, but we are striving not for the human nature but for the Divine, so let us fight the good fight and strive for peace with man as well as with God.

Dear Heavenly Father, please help me to develop the patience and love for others that will lead to harmony in my human relationships. I praise You for giving me inner peace in Your Holy Spirit. Help me to grow and show Your Light in my life.

PROVERBS 24:13,14 My son, honey whets the appetite, and so does wisdom! When you enjoy becoming wise, there is hope for you! A bright future lies ahead!

THE BEAR

The bear sure loves his honey,
And he can't stay away.
If he thinks there is a hive,
He's there without delay.

But he must use his knowledge.
In order to enjoy
The honeycomb of honey.
His brain he must employ.

The bear is quite an intelligent animal, and its strength is almost unbelievable. It can crush a man or rip an animal in two. This big creature is actually very fast, and although it may seem tame in certain areas (such as our national parks), it is not. We must use absolute discretion when visiting places where bears are seen. The bear is really a patsy for honey, sometimes lusting too anxiously for the sweet for its own good. It ends up with more trouble than it counted on! Sometimes we too are that way. We hunger for "honey" of one kind or another, and then that craving becomes primary. We forget everything and everyone else. It can lead to heartache and destruction. Let us try to use wisdom and moderation in our decisions.

Dear Heavenly Father, help me to use my head as well as my heart. Lest my earthly appetites lead me in the wrong direction, help me to examine my heart, mind, and soul before making any decision, no matter how small.

HEBREWS 12:15b Watch out that no bitterness takes root among you, for as it springs up it causes deep trouble, hurting many in their spiritual lives.

THE CENTIPEDE

The centipede is an invertebrate
With many agile feet.
He is a speedy predator,
And at night he likes to eat.

His front pair of legs are pincers,
Poisoning his prey.
This creature is mostly nocturnal,
And in daylight, he hides away.

There are countless species,
But you rarely see them at all.
Some grow quite large in the tropics,
But the ones we see are small.

While the centipede can grow to a length of ten and a half inches in Brazil, the ones we see are generally one to two inches long. They immobilize their prey by injecting poison into its system. Just as this poison paralyzes the centipede's prey, so bitterness can immobilize us. How can we grow spiritually with poison eating away at our hearts? The devil loves to work in insidious ways, and bitterness is one of his favorite tools. Once rooted, it grows like a cancer, affecting us and all of those with whom we come in contact. Let us be on the lookout for the first symptoms and escape by mobilizing our defenses—the Holy Spirit and God's mighty Word.

Dear Heavenly Father, I pray that I might be so filled with Your Spirit that no room is left in my heart for adverse feelings such as bitterness and resentment. I thank You for Your many blessings, knowing that under Your care and guidance I am free to reject such poisonous feelings.

PROVERBS 18:17 Any story sounds true until someone tells the other side and sets the record straight.

THE CLIMBING PERCH

In far-off Southeast Asia
Lives a fish beyond compare—
He swims like other fish do,
But his talent is quite rare!

This fish travels over land,
And he can move from pond to pond.
He survives out of water,
Though of water he is fond.

Natives carry him
As a fresh fish supply.
And he is often snapped up
By birds just passing by.

Yes, the climbing perch is unique. It was thought for many years that it could climb trees to suck the juices, but research has proven different. The fish found in trees have been dropped there by birds. This strange creature has an accessory breathing organ in the upper gill chamber that allows it to live out of water for some time. It is on overland journeys from pool to pool that birds find the perch an easy prey. The gill covers are rough and spiny and are used as "legs" in the fish's travels. Just as people accepted the tree-climbing concept as truth for years—on circumstantial evidence—we are tempted at times to believe exactly what we hear, with no concrete evidence to back it up. Oh, how many people have been hurt and misjudged by well-meaning storytellers! We must be very careful to hear both sides of any story before we have anything to say about it at all.

Dear Lord, help me to remember the climbing perch when I am tempted to make a judgment or pass along a story. I pray that I may be very careful of my witness and that I may make certain I know what I am talking about before I talk at all!

ROMANS 8:5 Those who let themselves be controlled by their lower natures live only to please themselves, but those who follow after the Holy Spirit find themselves doing those things that please God.

THE DRAGONFLY

The evil-looking insect
That we call the dragonfly,
The "devil's darning needle,"
Or "snake doctor," is not shy.

He'll gratify his hunger—
And his appetite is vast.
When he spots his dinner,
He is very, very fast.

He thinks of himself,
And gluttony is his creed.
Wherever there is food,
That's where he flies to feed.

This strange insect is truly a bloodthirsty creature. It has been called "the devil's darning needle," "horse stinger," and "snake doctor," among other names. From the time it is newly hatched and on into adulthood, it is ravenous. It will even eat its fellow dragonflies. It can consume enormous quantities and never seem to be full. If you bend its tail around to its mouth, it will even begin eating itself! The dragonfly will destroy itself through its very gluttony for it is truly controlled by its appetite. We too can be controlled by our earthly appetites if we allow it, and the path leads to destruction. But if we let the Holy Spirit work in our lives and if we live for Christ, we will find a life of peace and joy.

Dear Father in Heaven, I pray that I might learn to control my baser nature and live a life of right-doing, sharing Your love and blessings with all I meet. Help me to be known as "Christian" and to always reflect Your love and grace.

I PETER 2:1–3a So get rid of your feelings of hatred. Don't just pretend to be good! Be done with dishonesty and jealousy and talking about others behind their backs. Now that you realize how kind the Lord has been to you, put away all evil, deception, envy and fraud.

THE FLAMINGO

The flamingo is a beautiful bird,
With plumage of pink, black and red.
No other large bird is so colorful,
From the tip of his tail to his head.

He is from three to six feet long,
With long legs and big, webbed feet.
He has a long, sinuous neck,
And a bill that is structured to eat.

This strange bill is bent in the middle.
He's equipped with a filter device.
The good food is retained by the bird—
The bad is gone in a thrice!

Flamingos are aquatic birds and are very gregarious. They flock together in enormous numbers. There are several species, and while they vary in size, each feeds by a filtering system. The bill is structured so that water and mud are sucked into it, the good food is retained by the bird, and the unwanted material is rejected. Why don't we use this filtering system for ourselves? Let us keep the good—honesty, love, compassion, forgiveness—and filter out the bad—hatred, dishonesty, jealousy, all of the evil traits that destroy the soul. Our filtering system is powered by the Holy Spirit, and if we will just let it work in our lives, how happy and healthy we will be!

Dear Heavenly Father, it is wonderful to know that we can be free of sinful feelings! When evil thoughts enter our minds, we can simply filter them out, washed away by the blood of Jesus. I praise You for Your love!

MATTHEW 6:22,23 If your eye is pure, there will be sunshine in your soul. But if your eye is clouded with evil thoughts and desires, you are in deep spiritual darkness. And oh, how deep that darkness can be!

THE GALAGO

The soft and furry bush baby,
With its great, enormous eyes,
Has many cousin species,
And they vary in weight and size.

The dwarf weighs just two ounces,
With the largest the size of a hare—
But they all have those big, bright eyes,
And that deep, penetrating stare.

They have a strange attraction,
And it's easy to see why—
This small animal of Africa
Emits a baby's cry.

The name "bush baby" comes from the screeching noise the galago makes, much like the cry of an infant. It is related to the loris but has larger ears and a longer tail. Its senses are keen, and it folds its large ears up when sleeping. It is an insect eater. The "bush baby" is a very lovable-looking creature. Its big eyes invite our attention. We seem to look into its very heart. There is an old expression that says, "The eyes are the windows of the soul." Surely this seems to be true. Our eyes reveal our feelings. Hurt, anger, jealousy, love—all these show in our eyes. Let us try to keep our eyes as pure and bright as the galago's.

Dear Lord, I pray that my heart and soul might be so full of You that there is no room for the darkness of sin. I want only to be filled with the sunlight of Your love that others may see a reflection of You in my eyes.

PROVERBS 29:8 Fools start fights everywhere while wise men try to keep peace.

THE GIANT PANDA

The giant panda lumbers by,
Feeding on bamboo
In the Himalayan mountains
Or in the Washington zoo.

How can two hundred pounds
Look so cuddlesome?
Is he a bear or a raccoon?
Which family is he from?

He's strong and quite intelligent,
Yet he enjoys his play.
He's shy, and when he sees a man,
He runs and hides away.

The panda has long been in the public eye. There are very few in captivity, and those that are, are greatly loved and admired. Pandas are gentle and fun-loving for the most part. They are definitely not fools. We too should strive to be wise enough to keep the peace, to enjoy life, and to face calmly those who are contentious and fault-finding.

Dear Lord, I thank You for Your many blessings. I pray that I may be wise and try to keep the peace. When I feel my temper stirring, help me to pause and think of the consequences. Steer me away from the title of "fool."

JAMES 2:12,13 You will be judged on whether or not you are doing what Christ wants you to. So watch what you do and what you think; for there will be no mercy to those who have shown no mercy. But if you have been merciful, then God's mercy toward you will win out over his judgment against you.

THE GRASSHOPPER

The grasshoppers and locusts
Are related—every one.
There are six thousand species,
Living everywhere under the sun.

They have short antennae,
And most have two sets of wings—
(Although some species lack them)
They are used for the song they sing.

Their hind legs are large for jumping—
And jump they do, with glee.
They have large and compound eyes
To help these creatures see.

The grasshopper feeds entirely on grass and other plants. It is plain to see how it got its name. It is found in one form or another all over the world. The eggs are laid in the ground in a protective pod. A single pod will hold several hundred eggs. A few of the species are able to periodically multiply into vast, migrating swarms. These are known as locusts. They can cause mighty damage because they leave the trees and crops bare in their wake. In feeding themselves, they cause loss and destruction to other creatures. Sometimes we are like the locust, without meaning to be, especially when we hurt others by thinking only of ourselves. We must "do unto others," as Christ teaches. In showing mercy and compassion to others, we will receive that mercy and compassion from God on Judgment Day.

Dear Lord, help me to think of others first. Sometimes it is hard to follow Your will and Your way, but I pray that each step I take may build my strength so that I may hear the coveted words, "Well done," at the end of this life and the beginning of the next.

PROVERBS 31:30 Charm can be deceptive and beauty doesn't last, but a woman who fears and reverences God shall be greatly praised.

THE GREEN LACEWING

The lacewing is an insect
Of the Chrysopidae family—
A Greek word meaning "golden-eyed,"
And beautiful eyes has she.

They are large and iridescent,
And her wings attract our eye—
But "pretty is as pretty does,"
And those wings scarcely fly!

The lacewing is nocturnal—
She's not often seen by day.
Because her flight is weak and clumsy,
She often hides away.

The Lord has compensated,
And provided her with a smell.
When she is squeezed or just disturbed,
Her odor serves her well.

The filmy, veined wings that give this insect its name are really more ornamental than practical. They move with a slow, awkward flutter, making the lacewing easy prey in the daytime. Consequently, it is nocturnal. Once a predator kills a lacewing, however, it seldom tries again because of the unattractive odor that is emitted. The lacewing could do with less beauty in the wing department, and more practicality. We ourselves are much the same. Sometimes we place too much emphasis on outward charm and beauty and too little on the condition of the heart. If we concentrate on growing spiritually, we will not have to worry about charm and beauty—it will bloom naturally from within!

Dear Lord, help me to concentrate on the important things in life. I want always to be clean and neat and to present a good witness for You so that the beauty of the Spirit will show through. I pray that I might not let vanity and pride get a grip on me but that I might concentrate on the purity of You and Your Word.

PSALMS 51:10 Create in me a new, clean heart, O God, filled with clean thoughts and right desires.

THE HARVESTER

Daddy long-legs, can't you see
What your fate is going to be?
Legs so long, so fragile too—
They sometimes separate from you.
You have habits that are clean.
You wash each leg in turn, we've seen,
But then comes the dangerous part.
You wash your face, but when you start,
Many times you slip and falter
Through the top skim and into the water.
You often drown without a trace,
Losing your life to wash your face!

The daddy long-legs, or "harvester," is not from the spider family at all. This little creature moults its entire skin seven or eight times in its short life. If it loses a leg, the leg will not grow back as the spider's does. There are many sense organs on those long legs, so they must be kept cleared of dust and dirt. Consequently the daddy long-legs is meticulously clean. It washes each leg by pulling it through its jaws and then finds a pool of water to wash its face. It must put the first pair of legs on the surface film of the water in order to dip its mouth parts. Many times it breaks through and drowns. The daddy long-legs is a fanatic about cleanliness, even risking its life to be clean! We know that cleanliness is important to humans also, but the cleanliness that really counts dwells in our hearts. Although it is sometimes physically impossible to stay clean, we can always be clean mentally and spiritually.

Dear Heavenly Father, I pray that I may have a clean heart and mind at all times. Should I be tempted by evil thoughts, I need only turn to Your Word and I am refreshed and purified in thought and deed. Praise You!

PROVERBS 16:32 It is better to be slow-tempered than famous; it is better to have self-control than to control an army.

THE HIPPOPOTAMUS

An ugly thing, the hippo—
Enormous in size too.
He dearly loves the water,
And keeps it in his view.

He has a mild temperament,
And retreats from a fight.
He's also very curious,
And often not too bright.

He is an adept swimmer,
And like a log he'll float—
But when he is frightened,
He'll dive like a sinking boat!

The hippo, though homely, is a lovable creature. It can be enormous, standing from forty-eight to sixty-five inches at the shoulder and ranging from eleven to fifteen feet long. It may weigh from five thousand to eight thousand pounds. Yet it seems to be a calm and unexcitable creature. It loves the water and spends much of its time there, but—surprisingly—when on land, the hippo can outrun a man. Its barrel-bellied hulk and short, solid legs do not seem to hold it back, although they do make it appear quite awkward.

Dear Lord, I pray for the slow temper and self-control of the hippopotamus. Help me to stop and think lest I "fly off the handle," and teach me to have the inner peace that comes from reliance on You at all times.

PROVERBS 13:3 Self-control means controlling the tongue! A quick retort can ruin everything.

THE HORNED FROG

The horned frog sits
In a quiet heap,
So quietly
He could be asleep.

He'll carefully keep a watch
Until his meal's in view,
Then suddenly he will leap
As though by nature's cue.

He's named for horns
Above his eyes—
But his cavernous mouth
Is the big surprise!

The different species of horned frogs vary from bottle-cap to soup-bowl size. Its name is derived from the horns over the eyes of some species. Actually, it looks more like a toad than a frog. It has a large head, a blunt snout, and exceptionally wide jaws. When those jaws open, it often means trouble for something. But even small mouths can cause trouble. How often we open our mouths at the wrong time and say the wrong thing! Sometimes words just seem to leap out with no intention on our part at all. Self-control can be had only when the Lord is in control of self. It may be more accurate to use the term "Spirit-control" rather than "self-control."

Dear Heavenly Father, I pray for "Spirit-control" to guide me. I know that I need more control of self in every area of my life—speech, action, and thought. I pray that I may grow spiritually with the passing of each day—and that I may use Your dear Son as an example on my journey.

PROVERBS 13:20 Be with wise men and become wise. Be with evil men and become evil.

THE HOUSEFLY

The housefly carries myriads
And myriads of germs.
He is considered filthy
By our laboratory terms.

He cannot live in filth
And not spread it around—
Wherever the fly lands,
That same filthiness is found.

He may feast on garbage,
Then on our sugar bowl.
Bringing danger of disease,
He plays a villain's role.

Just as the common housefly carries the germs of the places it has been, so we carry the "germs" of our environment. We cannot be surrounded with evil without being affected by it. We may work and live in the midst of many who do not share our beliefs, but as long as we do so with the full armor of God and the protection of the Holy Spirit, we can remain pure at heart. We must be careful not to bring away "germs" of sin and wrong thinking with us but to strive to carry the sweetness of Christ to those who are not yet aware of it.

Dear Lord, help me to spread the Good News to those who have not heard. And I pray that I might be wrapped in Your love and grace as my protection in the face of evil.

PSALMS 94:8–10 Fools! Is God deaf and blind—he who makes ears and eyes? He punishes the nations—won't he also punish you? He knows everything—doesn't he also know what you are doing?

THE HYENA

Hear the hyenas'
Laughing cry,
And you'll know there's a meal
Somewhere nearby.

Their sight is poor,
But their smell is acute.
They are scavengers,
And far from mute.

They aren't afraid,
When in a pack,
To stalk big game,
And to attack.

What's said of them
Is seldom kind—
Their very name
Is much maligned!

There are three species of hyena—the spotted, or laughing, hyena, the striped hyena, and the brown hyena. The shoulders of all species are higher than the hind quarters, and they have an odd gait. They often hunt in packs and can run as fast as forty miles an hour. They have massive heads, large ears, and powerful jaws. Their teeth can easily shear through bone and muscle. They are far from attractive creatures, both in appearance and actions. Yet they are only animals, created to live for self. We are created in God's image, with a conscience and a soul. How, then, can we sin and expect Him to turn away and not notice? God is a loving God, but He is also a just God, and we will stand before him for His judgment of our life here on earth.

Dear Father, I love You and praise You. Help me to realize that You expect me to live a righteous life. You provide me with the Spirit, and I will be judged on my actions and thoughts. I pray that they may be pleasing to You.

ROMANS 15:5 May God who gives patience, steadiness, and encouragement help you to live in complete harmony with each other—each with the attitude of Christ toward the other.

THE KANGAROO

The kangaroo is an enigma—
It's hard to believe your eyes!
The animal is unbelievable,
A real mammalian surprise.

His delicate head and deerlike neck
Are graceful—but, dear me!
They slope down to heavy muscles,
And his haunches are awesome to see.

He has a thick and heavy tail,
It may be four feet long,
And he can leap twenty-five feet—
His hindquarters are that strong!

He may stand taller than a man,
And weigh two hundred pounds.
He loves to box, and often does—
He runs by leaps and bounds.

Kangaroos are peaceful animals, and very gregarious. They live in bands of from twenty to fifty members. They love to play, and their favorite sport is boxing. They do not fight to win, but for the fun of it. Although they rarely lose their tempers, they can be vicious if cornered. They graze together, wrinkling up their noses like rabbits and just enjoying the world around them. They would much rather use their strong hind legs to flee from trouble than for fight. Indeed, they are peace-loving and gentle animals.

Dear Lord, help me to seek peace and enjoyment in fellowship with my brothers and sisters. Give me the patience to understand others and the encouragement to help when I can. I thank You that we, Your children, can be happy together and content in Your love.

PROVERBS 27:7 Even honey seems tasteless to a man who is full; but if he is hungry, he'll eat anything!

THE KOMODO DRAGON

We read of prehistoric life,
And of mythology,
But this great creature lives today
On islands in the sea.

He's really a great lizard
And can grow to ten feet long,
But he's called the Komodo dragon
For the island he lives upon.

He may weigh three hundred pounds,
And his appetite's not small!
When this creature's hungry,
He'll eat anything at all!

The Komodo dragon's native home is in a few, small Indonesian islands—Komodo, Rintja, Flores, and Padar. Komodo is the largest, twenty miles by twelve miles, so you can see that they are all quite small. The Komodo dragon has a stout, flattened body with a long, thick neck and head. Its legs are short, with long claws on the toes. The long, narrow tongue constantly flicks in and out of the mouth. It can weigh as much as three hundred pounds. It will eat a heavy meal, gulping down large chunks, and then not eat again for days. When the Komodo dragon is hungry, it is not particular about its food—it will eat anything. Isn't it often the same with man? If we stay filled with the Spirit, we will not be led astray, but if a man is empty inside, he often turns to the wrong thing for fulfillment. Let us keep our hearts and minds on Christ so that we may never be spiritually hungry!

Dear Lord, I praise You! With You by my side, I need never thirst for I have the Living Water, and I need never hunger for I have Your Holy Word. Help me to share this wonderful news with others.

MARK 8:36,37 And how does a man benefit if he gains the whole world and loses his soul in the process? For is anything worth more than his soul?

THE PACK RAT

He's called a pack rat,
But he's really a vole.
You don't often see him—
He stays in his hole.

He has a blunt muzzle
And smallish eyes,
And his habits may come
As quite a surprise.

He doesn't just steal—
He trades what he finds.
When he takes something,
He leaves something behind.

The pack rat is about eighteen inches long, and half of that is tail. It weighs approximately three-quarters of a pound. There are twenty-two species found all over the world. They make complex nests, with many rooms, as they must have a place to store their treasures. They collect and hoard all sorts of objects, and the story is told of the pack rat that once stole worthless trinkets from a prospector's cabin and left gold nuggets in return. How foolish! And yet many of us are similarly tempted. We trade the love of Jesus and the everlasting life He offers for a few years of vain pleasure here and now. What a terrible, irreparable loss—a human soul!

Dear Heavenly Father, help me to keep my sights on the imperishable delights of Heaven and to be strong when it comes to resisting temptation. Help me to retain control and, with the aid of the Holy Spirit, walk with a firm step on this journey through life to Heaven.

PROVERBS 11:13 A gossip goes around spreading rumors, while a trustworthy man tries to quiet them.

THE PARROT

*A tropical bird, the parrot,
And most have strong, hooked beaks.
Some have a loud, harsh screeching,
And some have a high-pitched squeak.*

*They vary in size and color—
Some are very bright.
They can be tamed, and speak
If they are taught just right.*

*But parrots have a habit
Of repeating what they've heard.
They'll hear a conversation
And repeat every word!*

Yes, the parrot can be a very entertaining pet, but it can also be quite annoying and embarrassing. We can never be sure of what it might say or who it might say it to. Some people are similar. They listen to something that catches their interest and then, without thinking, they pass it on to someone else. Have you ever played the game called "Gossip"? Someone starts a story, and it is whispered around the room. It's amazing to see how that story changes and grows as it is passed from one person to another. Truly, gossip has no redeeming qualities! It causes only problems and trouble, and the best way to avoid it is for us to watch what we say and who we say it to in the first place.

Dear Heavenly Father, I pray that I may keep the dangers of gossip always in mind. Help me to refrain from participating in this popular "sport." If I have injured anyone through gossip, Lord, please forgive me and help me to be more careful. Words once spoken cannot be erased.

PROVERBS 4:7 Determination to be wise is the first step toward becoming wise! And with your wisdom, develop common sense and good judgment.

THE RATTLESNAKE

Beware the deadly rattlesnake—
His bite is venom-filled.
If you get too close to him,
You could be maimed or killed.

This creature gives a warning sign
Before that fatal strike—
You'll hear the buzzing of his rattles
Before his venom bite.

There are several different species
Of the rattlesnake.
They're active in the summertime,
In winter, they hibernate.

The rattlesnake has long been feared in the areas where it is found. Its bite is highly poisonous and can be fatal. And yet it almost invariably gives a warning before striking. The only exception is when it is in hiding. If we are wise and use common sense and good judgment, we need not fear the rattlesnake. The same is true with sin. We almost always have a warning "rattle" before we are "bitten" by sin. If we use our wisdom, common sense, and good judgment, we will escape before it has a hold on us. For indeed, sin is every bit as poisonous as the rattlesnake's venom—and it can be fatal to our very souls.

Dear Lord, help me to listen for that "warning rattle" and to recognize sin for what it is—a death trap. I pray for the wisdom to make the right choices on this road I travel toward You. I praise You and love You for Your constant Presence in my life.

JAMES 3:10–12 And so blessing and cursing come pouring out of the same mouth. Dear brothers, surely this is not right! Does a spring of water bubble out first with fresh water and then with bitter water? Can you pick olives from a fig tree, or figs from a grape vine? No—and you can't draw fresh water from a salty pool.

THE SHRIKE

We call the shrike a butcher-bird,
And here's the reason why.
Although the bird is small in size,
He shrieks with a killer's cry.

He may be a songbird,
Until he sees his prey—
But then his song soon changes,
And he is on his way.

He beats and pecks with his jagged bill
Until death has finally come,
Then hangs the prey from a handy thorn
And finds another one.

The shrike is a pleasant-looking little bird with a sweet song—but when it is hunting, its hooked and jagged beak is lethal. Its sweet song changes to a shrill squeal, and its killer instinct takes over. It is a bloody and cruel death for the prey, for the bird must beat and peck it to death. Just as the shrike changes from a sweet, unobtrusive songbird into a merciless killer, so we may be changed by anger, selfishness, envy—any one of our emotions. They can turn us from a loving human being into a hateful one. The shrike was created to live as it does, but we have a choice! We were created with freedom, and we must take responsibility for our actions. If we are full of the Spirit and feed on God's Word, there will be no room within us for the devil. Our negative emotions will be replaced by Christ's love.

Dear Father in Heaven, I pray that I might be increasingly filled with Your Spirit. Help me to commit my emotions to You, Lord, that with Your help, I might show forth love in every situation.

PROVERBS 25:18 Telling lies about someone is as harmful as hitting him with an ax, or wounding him with a sword, or shooting him with a sharp arrow.

THE STINGRAY

Stingrays like the ocean bed.
Searching for their prey,
They cover quite an area,
Undulating on their way.

When attacked or disturbed,
They lash out with their tail.
This brings the swordlike spine up
Toward the victim, without fail.

That spine is full of poison—
As its saw-toothed edges pierce.
It injects the venom
And causes pain most fierce!

The stingray has a disclike body with winglike fins. It measures from twelve inches to fourteen feet across and weighs from a pound and a half to seven hundred and fifty pounds. There are a hundred known species in temperate and tropical water. Each lives in shallow seas, seldom more than four hundred feet deep. If the stingray loses its spine, it grows another one, and sometimes another will grow while the first is still healthy, thus making the creature twice as dangerous. When the stingray pierces its prey with its poisonous spine, it can cause much agony and pain. We must remember that a lie can be just as injurious to its victim. It can hurt him mightily and may even fill him with the venom of hatred or bitterness. Let us be very careful of what we say about other people and make sure that what we say is proven fact. Even then, we must think twice before saying anything that might be harmful to someone else.

Dear Heavenly Father, before I let go a poison dart, I pray that I remember the hurt that might be inflicted on another—and to myself. Help me to reject the dart in the first place.

COLOSSIANS 3:11 In this new life one's nationality or race or education or social position is unimportant; such things mean nothing. Whether a person has Christ is what matters, and he is equally available to all.

THE STOAT

*The stoat hunts by scent
As he stalks his prey,
And though he's nocturnal,
He may hunt by day.*

*He's not particular—
Any flesh he will eat.
He is an expert hunter,
So does not lack for meat.*

*His body is long and supple,
His spine is agile too.
He twists and rolls and somersaults
In play, as animals do.*

*When winter brings its snow and ice—
It's worthy of a sermon—
This little brown creature turns to white,
And becomes a priceless ermine!*

The stoat, or short-tailed weasel as it is called in North America, is up to a foot in length, not counting the four-inch tail. The strangest thing about this creature is the change in it that cold weather brings. Its ordinary brown coat turns to white and is highly prized by hunters. It is known in its white state as ermine. Suddenly this ordinary animal is priceless! The Christian's worth is not determined by outside appearances but by the heart within. The world has many different standards. As with the hunters of the ermine, many people judge others by what is seen on the outside. Numerous social problems stem from this attitude. Race, education, and social position are too often the criteria by which the world judges us. God judges us by the heart, however, and as Christians, so must we!

Dear Heavenly Father, I pray that I might not be influenced by the outside appearance of another but only by what that person has done for Christ. Help me to be a good ambassador for You.

GALATIANS 5:25,26 If we are living now by the Holy Spirit's power, let us follow the Holy Spirit's leading in every part of our lives. Then we won't need to look for honors and popularity, which lead to jealousy and hard feelings.

THE TAHR

Tahr live in mountainous country
On craggy, rocky slopes.
The females prefer open hillside,
But the males know how to cope.

They climb the rocks and mountains
For ten months of the year,
And then they join the females
When breeding time is near.

Then these sure-footed animals
Let jealousy rear its head.
They fight and become careless,
And many end up dead.

Jealousy's a powerful tool,
And can bring a tahr to grief.
The cunning wiles of Satan
Are sometimes beyond belief!

Although the tahr is related to sheep and goats, they have odd characteristics all their own. There are three species: the Himalayan, the Arabian, and the Nilgiri. They are amazingly agile and sure-footed. They can jump as much as thirty feet to land on a narrow ledge below. They leap across ravines with ease. It is surprising, then, that these sure-footed creatures will sometimes let themselves be so off guard as to fall off a ridge or a cliff. This happens often during the mating season, when jealousy blinds them as they vie for the favor of the females. Jealousy can cause great unrest and trouble in our human relationships too. If we will just open ourselves to the Spirit of God, we will not have to worry about jealousy and popularity—for we will wish only the best for each other.

Dear Lord, the more I turn to You, the less important worldly things seem to be. And yet, as You take control of my life, I find that all my needs are filled—physically, spiritually, and intellectually. I thank You, Lord!

JAMES 3:5 So also the tongue is a small thing, but what enormous damage it can do. A great forest can be set on fire by one tiny spark.

THE WOODPECKER

The woodpecker specializes
With his tongue so long and thin—
It has adhesive on the tip
To reach larvae and ants for him.

He may be only six inches long,
Or he may be twenty-two.
There are several species
Of different shade and hue.

His voice is usually quite harsh,
And he often repeats.
It sounds like he is laughing,
Pecking for his treats!

Yes, woodpeckers are interesting birds. The tongue of some species extends a full two inches beyond the bill tip. It is used to extract ants, larvae, and other edibles from their hiding places. It spells nothing but trouble for the prey. Our tongues might not be so long in comparison—but they can cause deadly damage! The woodpecker has control of its tongue, but man does not always seem to have equal control. One statement—one word—can destroy a reputation or gravely hurt another's heart. Oh, to keep that tongue still and tending to the business it was made for! The tongue is the devil's greatest tool, and he uses it to advantage.

Dear Lord, I pray that I may learn to control my tongue and not be the one to light the spark to burn the forest. Help me to keep my tongue out of trouble—and out of other people's business. Remind me to *think* before I *speak*!

MATTHEW 5:21,22a Under the laws of Moses the rule was "If you kill, you must die." But I have added to that rule, and tell you that if you are only *angry*, even in your own home, you are in danger of judgment!

THE ZEBRA

Zebras seem peculiar
Because of their bright stripes.
The males are very aggressive,
And are often seen in fights.

They are potentially dangerous,
And even lions beware
If a zebra becomes enraged,
Although zebra's a favorite fare.

There are three species of zebra—
Grant's, Grevy's, and Burchell's.
The difference in size and markings
Is sometimes hard to tell.

The bright black and white of the zebra cannot be mistaken for anything else! Besides the stripes, however, there are several differences that set it apart from the horse and the ass. The skull and teeth are different as well as the "chestnuts"—hard, wartlike knobs on the legs. Also, the mane is upright and even. There are family groups under a stallion, and also bachelor herds. The biggest and strongest stallions often go off on their own. They may weigh up to a thousand pounds. They have a touchy temper and easily become enraged. We sometimes find it easy to lose our tempers too and lash out at others. Christ tells us that the thought is judged as well as the action. Let us strive to be calm and rein in that temper. Usually we find our anger wasn't worth it anyway.

Dear Lord, help me to stay in control when I become upset. I pray that I might show love rather than anger, no matter what the situation. Love is a winner—and temper is always a loser. The devil finds it one of his most useful tools. Help me to remember that.

7
Stewardship

PSALMS 119:73 You made my body, Lord; now give me sense to heed your laws.

THE AARDVARK

The aardvark has a heavy body,
Four feet long and two feet high.
"Earth pig" is another name
That this creature is known by.

He has a tail two feet in length,
And a muzzle like a pig.
His ears are really donkeylike—
They are pointed and quite big.

His sticky tongue is very long.
He has sharp claws on his feet.
Termites are his favorite food,
And he destroys their nests to eat.

The aardvark has no close living relatives. It is in a class by itself. It is called "tube-toothed" because of the fine tubes radiating through each tooth. The teeth are very unique as they have no roots or enamel, unlike any other animal. It is a burrower, and Africa is its habitat. This "earth pig" is a strange-looking creature, but its odd body is well adapted for the life it lives. It follows the course of nature, doing what it was intended to do. Are we doing as well? God has given us bodies that will serve us well if we use them as we should. Let us read the "instruction manual"—God's Word—and treat this body with respect, for it is a gift from Him. Let us use it as He intended us to.

Dear Father in Heaven, I thank You for this body you have provided for me. Help me to use it with respect, just as You would want me to. And help me to read and heed Your Word, Lord, so I will have nothing to be ashamed of when I meet You face to face!

ROMANS 13:12,13a The night is far gone, the day of his return will soon be here. So quit the evil deeds of darkness and put on the armor of right living, as we who live in the daylight should!

THE ARMADILLO

The strange armadillo,
When he can't avoid detection,
Will bend and close his armor
If in need of the protection.

One type, in Argentina,
Can clamp into a sphere.
He closes like a steel trap—
Not like the species here.

He is a heavy animal
And can walk beneath a pond,
Although he's a good swimmer
If that skill is called upon.

There are numerous species of the armadillo. Most of them live in South America, but the nine-banded armadillo reaches as far north as southern Kansas. The three-banded armadillo in Argentina can actually close up completely, like a steel trap. Most of the others can draw their feet and legs beneath the shell or roll into a ball so that their armor protects them from harm. If we will don the armor of Christian living, we too will be protected from potential harm. A life filled with Christ has no vacancy for the devil. We must constantly renew ourselves through study and prayer and keep our armor in good shape, with no weak spots for evil to penetrate. Predators have learned to flip the armadillo over and attack its soft spot. Let us protect our soft spots with prayer and the Holy Spirit!

Dear Heavenly Father, I praise You for the armor of right living you make available to me. Give me the strength and courage to put it on and wear it proudly in Your Name.

ISAIAH 30:21 And if you leave God's paths and go astray, you will hear a Voice behind you say, "No, this is the way; walk here."

THE BAT

The strange mammal called the bat
Has the ability to fly.
His wings are made of membrane
And will carry him quite high.

He has a sonar system
To help him locate prey.
It also guides around the things
That may get in his way.

There are thirteen hundred species
Of bat that man has found,
And around this unique creature,
Mysteries still abound.

Yes, the bat still holds many mysteries for man. Its breeding habits are being studied closely, along with its ability to adjust its body temperature. Its unique sonar system is more effective than any that man has been able to produce. As the bat has its "sonar system" to steer it away from trouble, so do we. The Holy Spirit nudges us from within, helping us divide right from wrong. But just as the bat must follow its instinctive guide, so we too must follow the Spirit's leading.

Dear Lord, thank You for equipping me with the "sonar" I need. Help me to be strong enough to follow as You guide me around the obstacles in my Christian walk. I love You and praise You.

EZEKIEL 33:4,5 Anyone who hears the alarm and refuses to heed it—well, if he dies the fault is his own. For he heard the warning and wouldn't listen; the fault is his. If he had heeded the warning, he would have saved his life.

THE BOXFISH

The boxfish has another name—
He's called the trunkfish too.
And all because he is enclosed
In bony plates—it's true.

Only the fins, the jaws, and tail
Are free to move at all—
The body is held rigid and straight
Inside its armored wall.

The boxfish has bright, vibrant colors
To warn the other fish.
You see, he is not edible—
He is a poisonous dish!

Many of the boxfish are colored with red, blue, and yellow combined in varying patterns. They grow up to twenty inches in length and secrete a virulent poison into the water that will kill other fish. Thus their bright coloration frightens off predators, which see the colors as an alarm denoting danger. We too have heard the alarm if we have read God's Word. If we heed the warning and find safety in Christ Jesus, we have nothing to worry about, but if we ignore the warning and live our lives with no thought of God, we are bound for sorrow and destruction—and the fault will be our own.

Dear Lord, help me to respond to the alarm system You have provided. I praise You for giving us the Word that allows us to make the choice between life and death—and to make it freely.

MATTHEW 28:19,20a Therefore, go and make disciples in all nations, baptizing them in the name of the Father and of the Son and of the Holy Spirit, and then teach these new disciples to obey all the commands I have given you.

THE BUZZARD

The buzzard, with his big, broad wings,
Is renowned for soaring flight—
And yet he perches on trees or rocks
To keep his prey in sight.

He feeds on ground mammals and reptiles,
But also eats carrion and such.
Of the several species known,
None are admired much.

The buzzard is a cousin
To the eagle and the hawk.
He's the family "ugly duckling"
As he sits upon his rock.

The vulture and buzzard are brothers,
And they have long been found
To do most of their hunting
Upon the solid ground.

The buzzard and vulture are often looked upon with disgust because they eat carrion, but this practice is actually very helpful to man. Of the entire family, including hawks and eagles, only five percent are potentially harmful, and when we study them closely, we find the harm that they do is negligible. The buzzard is especially known for its ability to fly high. Isn't it strange that this bird—renowned as it is for its high flights—goes to the ground for its food? And yet how often do we do the same thing? We find it much easier to witness to those far away than to our own families or our neighbors in close proximity. Let us not neglect to bring the Word to those close to us in our daily walk.

Dear Lord, help me to be a good witness to those nearby. Help me to realize that it is my responsibility to spread the Gospel near as well as far!

II TIMOTHY 2:25 Be humble when you are trying to teach those who are mixed up concerning the truth. For if you talk meekly and courteously to them they are more likely, with God's help, to turn away from their wrong ideas and believe what is true.

THE CARIBOU

The caribou, or reindeer,
Is equipped to live in snow.
He has broad hoofs that are concave
On the bottom to help him go.

The bulls are larger than the cows,
But each sex grows a rack—
A good big pair of antlers,
That are shed and then grow back.

This animal is silent,
And he never makes a sound—
Even when he's showing off,
He silently paws the ground.

The bull has a mane, and a full-grown caribou will vary in height from forty-two inches to fifty inches at the shoulder. It is brown with pale gray on the neck. The gray turns to white in the winter. It is well equipped to weather through the ice and snow. It is found in both the Western and Eastern Hemispheres, being called "caribou" in North America and "reindeer" in the East. Even during rut, these animals are vocally silent. But we cannot be silent. We must use our voices to teach the truth. Let us always use them in the right way, being kind and courteous in all we say. If we speak the truth with a loving heart, we will be heard and listened to. The truth cannot be taught by force—only by reason.

Dear Lord, help me to give full rein to the Holy Spirit and to follow the example You set in Your teaching. Let me be truthful, sincere and loving, that those who hear might believe and accept You as Savior.

PSALMS 4:1 O God, you have declared me perfect in your eyes; you have always cared for me in my distress; now hear me as I call again. Have mercy on me. Hear my prayer.

THE CHUCKWALLA

An iguana called the chuckwalla
Makes his home in Mexico.
He's a heavy-bodied reptile
With strong legs to make him go.

He attains a length of twelve inches—
He's plump, with a long, slender tail.
This creature is herbivorous,
With a coat made up of scales.

The chuckwalla has a habit—
He can inflate his lungs, and soon
He can be safely wedged in a crevice,
By inflating like a balloon!

The chuckwalla feeds on fruits and the flowers of the cactus in the desert regions of northern Mexico and the southwestern United States. It has the strange ability to inflate its lungs so that its body is almost ball-like. When the chuckwalla is frightened, it runs into a crevice and inflates. It is almost impossible to extract it from its hiding place. God takes care of the chuckwalla in a way that man would not dream of. Even this little animal is perfect in God's sight. He has declared us perfect too, and any imperfections we have are the result of what we ourselves have done to a perfect creation. Our Father listens to our pleas for help and will always have mercy and compassion on us if we but ask.

Dear Lord, I thank You, my Creator, for my life. I pray that You will forgive me for my wrongful actions and have mercy on me, a sinner. I love You, Lord, for I know that You first loved me.

ISAIAH 29:15 Woe to those who try to hide their plans from God, who try to keep him in the dark concerning what they do! "God can't see us," they say to themselves. "He doesn't know what is going on!"

THE COCKROACH

The cockroach is a creature
That man abominates.
He's old as old as he can be—
As pest, he dominates.

The very name spells "horror!"
It brings out spray and brush.
It's hard to catch the cockroach
For he's always in a rush.

He looks on light as danger,
And scurries out of sight.
He sleeps during the daylight hours,
And hunts for food at night.

Ask any homemaker and she will tell you the cockroach is an "abomination." And indeed the household species is just that. However, the cockroach is being used in space and medical research because of its hardy nature. Just as the cockroach hides from the light, so do many Christians. We must realize that truly we cannot hide from God. He knows what we do before we even do it, and He knows our very minds. Accepting Christ as Savior is not enough—that is only the first step. We must accept Him as Lord of our lives and live for Him. When we do that, we will want to walk in the light—as children of the King!

Dear Heavenly Father, help me to think less often of myself and more of You. I thank You and praise You for giving me Your Word to live by. With it, I can leave the darkness of sin behind and live in the Light of the Son.

JAMES 5:16 Admit your faults to one another and pray for each other so that you may be healed. The earnest prayer of a righteous man has great power and wonderful results.

THE CROW

In the field you hear the chattering cry
As a flock of crows comes flying by.
They swoop down on the fresh-sown wheat
With bobbing beaks and busy feet.

The crow can be a farmer's pest,
But he can also be the best—
He'll rob the seed, I know that's true—
But he'll rid the field of insects too.

He can talk when he is tamed—
He even treats it like a game.
Yes, the crow has two sides too—
Much the same as me or you!

The typical crow is of the corvid family. There are many species, both in Europe and the Americas. The ones we usually see are black and have a metallic gloss in the sunlight. They are scavengers and will eat almost anything. They are highly intelligent birds and very gregarious. Their cry is harsh and unmusical. It is thought that they mate for life. The crow can be a pest, but he can also be a great help to agriculture.

Dear Lord, help me to ever strive to increase my good qualities and decrease the bad. Teach me to share with my Christian brothers and sisters in prayer—that we might give strength to each other through Your great storehouse of love.

GALATIANS 1:8 Let God's curses fall on anyone, including myself, who preaches any other way to be saved than the one we told you about; yes, if an angel comes from heaven and preaches any other message, let him be forever cursed.

THE DOUROUCOULI

These South American monkeys
Make noises both soft and strong—
From the roaring of a jaguar
To a baby kitten's song.

They're also known as owl monkeys
Because of their large eyes.
They are nocturnal creatures,
And they're agile and small in size.

When they sleep in the daytime,
They roll into a ball of fur.
They may be little monkeys,
But their messages cause a stir!

The douroucouli is also known as the owl monkey, or night monkey. Its size ranges from nine and a half to fourteen and a half inches, with a tail of equal length. It can make unbelievably loud and resonant calls. It has a repertoire of about fifty calls, ranging from incredibly loud to as soft as a kitten's meow. It can move through the trees in absolute silence, never making a sound. Its habitat is the rain forests of South America. The douroucouli may have fifty messages, but as Christians, we have just one. The only way to eternal life is through Jesus Christ, the Son of God. He was born of a virgin, died on the cross for our transgressions, and rose on the third day. Let us strive to spread the Gospel to all we meet!

Dear Heavenly Father, what a wonderful message we have! Help us to share the Gospel news that while the physical self lasts for only a few years, the spiritual self is eternal. Teach me to be a swift messenger for You.

COLOSSIANS 3:17 And whatever you do or say, let it be as a representative of the Lord Jesus, and come with him into the presence of God the Father to give him your thanks.

THE FIRE-BELLIED TOAD

The fire-bellied toad
Is really a frog within—
When you see him from above
He has a gray, warty skin.

But that skin is poisonous,
And will make you sneeze and itch.
This frog's found throughout Europe,
In many a pool or ditch.

If he is disturbed
And can't seem to get away,
He arches back so you can see
His red-belly display.

Bombina, the true fire-bellied toad, is a frog with a dull gray skin full of warts, but its stomach is vividly patterned with bright red. It displays this bright color as a warning of danger. Bombina spends most of its time in the water, hanging motionless with only its snout and eyes above the surface. However, if it is disturbed, it swims well with its webbed toes. Its poisonous skin produces a frothy, irritating liquid. It leaves the water in winter and hibernates in a burrow. The fire-bellied toad displays its colors as a warning, but let us display our colors as witnesses for Christ. We are just like everyone else on the outside, but the Spirit of God should shine out brightly from within for all to see.

Dear Heavenly Father, I want to be a positive representative for Christ and the Christian way of life. I pray that I may show at all times the colors of love, truthfulness, and compassion.

MARK 16:15,16 And then he told them, "You are to go into all the world and preach the Good News to everyone, everywhere. Those who believe and are baptized will be saved. But those who refuse to believe will be condemned.

THE FRILLED LIZARD

This agamidae lizard
In New Guinea and Australia is found.
You may see him on a tree trunk
Or scampering over the ground.

His colors are not fantastic,
But he may be three feet long—
Of course that's counting a long tail.
He's big, but not too strong.

This lizard is named for a frill
That folds back from the neck.
When he's alarmed, he opens his mouth,
And brings the frilled collar erect.

The color of the frilled lizard is not spectacular. It varies from a russet or gray to a near-black. The stomach may be white or brick red, with a black throat and chest. It is not a desert lizard for it likes trees. The frilled ruffle around the neck opens like an umbrella by the tongue-bone extensions. Just as the ruffle is erected when the lizard opens its mouth, so the Holy Spirit should be activated when we open ours. No matter what we say, if it is in a Christian manner, the Good News will come through. Never be shy or afraid to speak out for Christ. It may mean the difference between spiritual life and death to the person you are talking with.

Dear Father in Heaven, sometimes witnessing with words can be the hardest task in the world. Give me the strength and courage to do it and to do it well, knowing that I have the most important message a person can bear to the world.

TITUS 2:7 And here you yourself must be an example to them of good deeds of every kind. Let everything you do reflect your love of the truth and the fact that you are in dead earnest about it.

THE GARPIKE

The garpike lies in the water,
Close to the weedy floor.
He really is quite lazy,
And easy to ignore.

And yet if he is after food,
He has a burst of speed.
He never uses more energy
Than he really needs.

The surface of his body
Is like a fine mosaic—
Each scale fits so perfectly,
The pattern never breaks.

The garpike is found in fresh waters in the southeastern parts of North America. The anal and dorsal fins are set far back on the body for bursts of speed when needed. However, the garpike is an essentially lazy creature and spends most of its time among the weeds. The scales of the garpike are lovely to see, and they are sometimes made into jewelry. They are diamond-shaped, and unlike those of other fish, they do not overlap but are fitted together like a mosaic into a pattern of beauty. We too should be like a pattern of beauty to those around us, the pieces fitting together perfectly without a break in a Christian life of love. We must often work on the pieces to make them fit smoothly, but we have all the help we need from the Lord.

Dear Heavenly Father, help me to be a pattern worthy of You. I pray that You will weave a tapestry of beauty out of my life so that others may see Your marvelous workmanship.

ROMANS 15:4 These things that were written in the Scriptures so long ago are to teach us patience and to encourage us, so that we will look forward expectantly to the time when God will conquer sin and death.

THE GERENUK

It once was thought this creature
Was a strange type of gazelle.
He's found in Ethiopia,
Somalia, and Kenya as well.

His neck is very, very long,
And he feeds on his hind feet,
Reaching higher branches
When he wants the leaves to eat.

When water is available,
He drinks to his heart's delight,
But he survives for quite some time
Without a drink in sight.

The gerenuk has also been known as the giraffe-necked gazelle and Waller's gazelle. However, it is not of the gazelle family at all. It is excessively shy. It lives singly or in pairs in Ethiopia, Somalia, and northern Kenya. Sometimes several will form a small herd of from three to ten—seldom more. They have the ability to go without water for prolonged periods, perhaps because they conserve what water they do drink. We should drink from God's Word whenever it is available and commit portions to memory for the dry times when we cannot read. What a source of strength, patience, and encouragement it is. When we are filled with the Living Water, we know no thirst!

Dear Father in Heaven, help me to exercise my brainpower by memorization of Your Word—even though it will be difficult because of the many distractions in the world today. I know that memorization is fast becoming a lost art, but I need to know Your Word at all times for witnessing and for helping others—as well as for my own dry times.

HEBREWS 4:13 He knows about everyone, everywhere. Everything about us is bare and wide open to the all-seeing eyes of our living God; nothing can be hidden from him to whom we must explain all that we have done.

THE GLASSFISH

The glassfish may be small in size,
But he's notable in his way—
His body is clearly transparent;
You can see bones and vertebrae.

You can't see through the stomach
And he has an opaque head,
But otherwise he hides nothing—
He's as clear as glass instead.

The glassfish lives in the fresh waters of Burma, Thailand, and India. It is a small, stocky fish about three inches long with two dorsal fins. Its body is so clear that you can see the entire bone structure. There is a silvery covering over the stomach, but otherwise the whole body is completely transparent. We may not be transparent to other people, but, oh—we are to God! He knows all about us . . . everything we do . . . everything we think. Let us strive to be pure through and through that we might never be ashamed.

Dear Heavenly Father, I know that You see my every thought. I pray that I might be pleasing to You and never grieve You. Help me to be truly sincere in all things to all people and—most of all, Lord—to You.

GENESIS 1:31a Then God looked over all that he had made, and it was excellent in every way.

THE GREEN TURTLE

The green turtle is a big fellow—
He'll weigh a thousand pounds,
Although he's usually smaller than that
When observed in his home grounds.

This turtle has a problem—
He tastes so good, you see,
He's hunted for his meat and eggs—
For his palatability!

Scientists have noted this,
And they have taken steps
To save him from extinction
So that he can roam the depths.

The green turtle, like so many of God's creatures, is in danger of extinction. It is hoped that through care and planning this situation can be rectified. Why doesn't man use more care in the first place? As caretakers of God's creatures, we should use moderation. He has provided us with many sources of food—let us use them by need, not greed.

Dear Heavenly Father, help us to restore the balance of nature. We have made many mistakes, but I—as one person—will do my part to rectify them. Teach me to keep before me the questions: "Will this hurt my environment?" "Will this harm God's Creation?" I know that many times the answer will be "yes." Teach me to listen and act accordingly.

MATTHEW 7:24–27 All who listen to my instructions and follow them are wise, like a man who builds his house on solid rock. Though the rain comes in torrents, and the floods rise and the storm winds beat against his house, it won't collapse, for it is built on rock. But those who hear my instructions and ignore them are foolish, like a man who builds his house on sand. For when the rains and floods come, and storm winds beat against his house, it will fall with a mighty crash.

THE HAMMERHEAD

A peculiar bird—the hammerhead—
With large eyes and a spadelike bill.
He has a crest upon his head
That he can move at will.

He eats like other water birds,
He likes fish and frogs.
He also catches insects
In his favorite marshy bogs.

His home is quite a castle—
Though it's built with sticks,
It's fortified with mud and moss—
Its walls are one foot thick.

The bird is twenty inches long,
And his body is stout,
And yet the door to his abode
Leaves six inches to get in or out!

The hammerhead is like a heavily built heron but is in a class of its own. It gets its name from its crest, which resembles the claws of a hammer. It builds its nest near the water on a cliff or in the fork of a tree. The walls may be one foot thick and the roof over a yard thick—well able to take the weight of a man or the pounding of the heaviest storm. The only way the hammerhead can enter is to plummet straight into the nest, folding its wings tight against its body. It truly builds a fortress. Many other creatures covet its home because of its safety. We too must build a solid house on a firm foundation, and what firmer foundation is to be had than Jesus Christ and His Word?

Dear Lord, please help me to follow Your instructions and build a strong house on a firm foundation. I pray that I may be prepared for the storms of life and that I may weather them through and come out victorious—with Your Word in my heart and hand.

LUKE 10:2 These were his instructions to them: "Plead with the Lord of the harvest to send out more laborers to help you, for the harvest is so plentiful and the workers so few."

THE HARVEST MOUSE

The yellowish-red harvest mouse
Has underparts of white.
He lives in three-hour cycles
Throughout the day and night.

He sleeps until the third hour,
When he takes the time to feed—
Then he goes to sleep again
In his nest of grass and weeds.

He likes the cereal crops,
And lives there when he can.
He waits there 'til the harvest,
When he must start again.

This attractive little mouse builds its nest of shredded grass blades. The staple diet is seeds, especially those of grasses and grains, so the nest is usually in the fields. It is circular and can be found hanging between stalks of grass or grain. This little creature is about five inches in length, counting the tail, and weighs about a quarter of an ounce. It loses its dainty nest when the grain is harvested and must build a new home. Just as this tiny mouse waits for the harvest, so do we. Of course we have different reasons. Mr. Harvest Mouse waits for it because he knows his home will need rebuilding. We watch for opportunities to *work* in the harvest fields—to sow the Word and help reap new souls for Christ. When the time is right, we too will have a new home—in Heaven!

Dear Father in Heaven, help me to get busy in the harvest fields and win more souls for Thee. There are many who do not yet know the Good News of the Gospel. Teach me to reach them and bring them to a saving knowledge of Christ.

II TIMOTHY 4:6–8 I say this because I won't be around to help you very much longer. My time has almost run out. Very soon now I will be on my way to heaven. I have fought long and hard for my Lord, and through it all I have kept true to him. And now the time has come for me to stop fighting and rest. In heaven a crown is waiting for me which the Lord, the righteous Judge, will give me on that great day of his return. And not just to me, but to all those whose lives show that they are eagerly looking forward to his coming back again.

THE JELLYFISH

Imagine an open umbrella
With no handle but a mouth
Surrounded by many tentacles,
Floating east, west, north, and south.

There are many jellyfish
In different areas of the sea—
All of them are strange creatures,
And live their lives floating free.

Their substance is not a solid state—
Some are venomous to the touch.
They are ninety-nine percent jelly,
And five percent organic, as such.

If they wash up from the ocean
And lay upon the drying sand,
They will vanish in the sunlight
As if a magician used sleight of hand.

The size of jellyfish varies from minute to six feet across the main body. The creature swims by rhythmic pulsations of the "umbrella." Its nervous system and sense organs are simple. Some jellyfish—those known as sea wasps—are capable of a venomous sting that may sometimes bring death. When the jellyfish dies, it leaves nothing behind, since it is almost completely composed of water. We die to go to our Lord, to live with Him in Heaven. As Christians, we should leave behind a life of witness for Him. Just think! Even after our physical deaths, we can continue witnessing for Him through our actions while here on earth!

Dear Lord, I pray that my witness may be such that it will influence people for You—not only today but even after I am physically gone. If I can influence one single soul for You, I will feel that I have fulfilled my purpose.

JOHN 12:37 But despite all the miracles he had done, most of the people would not believe he was the Messiah.

THE KINGFISHER

The kingfisher's reputation
Is not exactly true—
He does not build a nest of bones
Or spear his prey on cue.

He's only six and a half inches long—
A dumpy little bird.
The stories told about him
Are really quite absurd!

He watches from a tree above
Until he spots his prey.
Then he dives with open beak,
And catches the fish away.

She lays her eggs on bare soil,
And the fishbones, as she eats,
Accumulate around the eggs,
Surrounding her bright red feet.

A strange story is often easy to believe, and so it is with the stories told of the kingfisher. Since this small bird has a long, sharp bill, the story of stabbing its victims is not hard to understand. The story of a nest built of bones is easy to believe also when the bones are found around the eggs. We really do not need much coaxing to believe what we want to believe. Then why is it sometimes so hard for us to accept what we know to be truth? There are millions of people today who still reject the truth of the Gospel. Why? Because belief demands a commitment—a commitment to Christ and the Christian way of life, a release of self to God.

Dear Heavenly Father, I accept Your Word as truth. I pray that I may keep my eternal commitment to You. It brings peace of mind and a life of purpose and meaning. I praise You for the truth that has set me free!

MATTHEW 4:5-7 Then Satan took him to Jerusalem to the roof of the Temple. "Jump off," he said, "and prove you are the Son of God; for the Scriptures declare, 'God will send his angels to keep you from harm,' . . . they will prevent you from smashing on the rocks below." Jesus retorted, "It also says not to put the Lord your God to a foolish test!"

THE KITTIWAKE

Kittiwakes build a small, stout nest
Made of mud and grass.
They prefer a ledge or cliff,
And make their nest to last.

The kittiwake actually is a gull,
But smaller than his brothers.
He feeds on fish and plankton,
And won't steal eggs like the others.

The young ones are watched carefully
As they eat and grow.
They must not fall off the cliff
Onto the rocks below.

The kittiwake is small, about sixteen inches long. It gets its name from its call, "kitt-i-waak." It lives in the North Atlantic Ocean, and one species, the red-legged kittiwake, breeds in the Bering Sea and the North Pacific. Kittiwakes spend most of their time at sea, where they usually feed by plunge-diving. Toward the end of May or June, they appear on the coasts to nest in large colonies. They build sturdy nests on the narrowest cliffs and ledges they can find. They watch their new chicks carefully lest they fall off the edge of the cliff. We too should watch our step, showing responsibility in our actions. The Lord is always there to help us when we need Him, but let's not put Him to the test unnecessarily.

Dear Lord, I thank You for your help when I need it, and I pray that I may exercise my intelligence and live my life in a responsible manner. Help me to stay away from the edge of the cliff, Lord, and safe within Your will.

EPHESIANS 5:1 Follow God's example in everything you do just as a much loved child imitates his father.

THE LEAF FISH

The leaf fish lives in the Amazon,
And his camouflage is great!
He lives on the still-water bottoms
In the weeds—he and his mate.

He digs a hole to make a nest,
And she then comes to court.
The male fish watches over the eggs—
The hatching time is short.

These fish are three to eight inches long,
And flattened side to side.
They really do resemble a leaf,
As in the plants they hide.

The camouflage of the leaf fish is truly remarkable. It usually lives in still or slow-moving waters, where it blends perfectly with the water-plant leaves. There are several species in South America. The leaf fish can swallow another fish three-quarters of its own size, and normally it eats its weight in food each day. It follows the example of the water plants around it—from its appearance to its actions. It will position itself in such a way as to be completely undetectable. It is taken to be a leaf! Oh, if only we could be as good at imitation as this little fish! Let us try to follow God's example in everything we do, that others might see God in us.

Dear Heavenly Father, what a beautiful example You give me! Please help me to follow the pattern You lay out. Help me to grow in the Spirit until people no longer see me, but You in me.

PROVERBS 25:19 Putting confidence in an unreliable man is like chewing with a sore tooth, or trying to run on a broken foot.

THE LUMPSUCKER

There can hardly be another
With such fatherly devotion!
We're talking about the lumpsucker,
And his constant guardian motion.

The female lays thousands of eggs
Between the water lines.
At high tide they are covered,
And at low tide left behind.

The lumpsucker gets his name
From the strong sucker made of fins.
He can cling to almost anything—
His tenacity usually wins!

The male watches over the tiny eggs—
He'll attach himself nearby
And aerate the eggs, no matter what,
Even though he may die.

There is an eight-month period of fasting observed by the lumpsucker. From April to November, the breeding season, the stomach is distended with water. This strange fish, up to two feet long, is a great example of parental devotion. The male will guard the eggs with its very life. This is its natural instinct, and there may be up to 136,000 pink eggs under its care. It is truly reliable. We, too should be reliable in whatever task we undertake. As Christians, we should be known for our reliability and for being true to our word. We must be careful not to promise more than we can deliver!

Dear Lord, help me to be reliable and dependable as a witness to You. I realize that everything I do is a witness, either for or against the Christian way of life. I pray that my witness may be a positive influence in winning more souls for You.

PSALMS 67:2,3 Send us around the world with the news of your saving power and your eternal plan for all mankind. How everyone throughout the earth will praise the Lord!

THE LYREBIRD

In mountain forests where rocky slopes
Run down and the waters play,
That is where the lyrebirds
Act out their unique display.

The male sings and dances, his lacy tail
A shimmering canopy.
His song is strong and beautiful,
His tail shakes violently.

Then he cuts short the bubbling notes,
His tail folds and he walks away.
He has established his territory
In one glorious, fine display!

The lyrebird has a body about the size of a bantam rooster, with strong legs and feet. Its tail is made up of sixteen feathers and extends to a two-foot length. The two outer feathers are broad and shaped like the frame of a lyre, while the remaining feathers fill the framework with delicate, lacy plumes. It has a beautiful voice and can mimic many bird calls and sounds. It uses its display and song to establish its territory, which ranges from three to six acres. Our territory is much broader. The Bible tells us to go to all the world with our song—the Gospel message!

Dear Heavenly Father, help me to convey the Good News wherever I go and in everything I do and say. I want to sing the sweet song of love and redemption for all who will hear and to display the results of Your Spirit in my life!

GENESIS 1:21,26 So God created great sea creatures, and every sort of fish and every kind of bird. And God looked at them with pleasure, and blessed them all. Then God said, "Let us make a man—someone like ourselves, to be the master of all life upon the earth and in the skies and in the seas."

THE MANATEE

The sweet song of the mermaid,
Heard by men of old,
Is thought to be from the manatee,
Or so I have been told.

The manatee, or sea cow,
May weigh a half a ton.
A mammal, living in the water,
He is a gentle one.

Though his size is awesome,
His actions are usually mild—
He grazes on water hyacinths,
Innocently, as a child.

He trusts other creatures—
Is a good neighbor too.
The manatee, it's plain to see,
Does as we should do!

These huge giants of the water world are not attractive to look at, but their gentle way of living draws us to them. Every few minutes they must surface to breathe, and they are strangely graceful for their size. They go along minding their own business, bothering no one. And yet their greatest enemy is man—man with his speedboats and fishing spears. The manatee stays close to the surface and is often injured by motor blades or mistaken for game fish. Many of those observed have been badly scarred. Why don't we have more respect for God's creatures?

Dear Lord, please help me to be a good steward of Your creatures, for every creation of Yours is worthy of the care and respect of men. Help me to impress this thought on others. May I, this day, look for You in all I see in this world around me.

PROVERBS 15:28 A good man thinks before he speaks; the evil man pours out his evil words without a thought.

THE MOLE

The mole is an interesting animal
Living underground.
His eyes have a protective covering,
And he hears loud sounds.

His front feet are adapted
For digging in the dirt—
He leaves a telltale ridge,
Although he doesn't hurt.

He's almost always hungry
And eats insect pests,
Like cutworms and beetle larvae,
That garden plots infest.

His ridges are unsightly,
But they do aerate the soil,
And make it more productive
For the gardener's toil.

This little mammal, seven to nine inches long from nose to tail tip, is really a help to man. Its tunnels are very clean, and it eats as it digs. If the tunnels are too close to the surface, they will leave a ridge in their wake. Consequently, one of its chief enemies is man. If we would weigh the bad and the good the mole does, the scales would tip considerably to the good side. However, man often speaks and acts before he thinks.

Dear Lord, I pray that I might think first and act later. So much harm can be done by thoughtless words and actions, and people can be hurt—innocent people who are trying hard to do their best. Help me to pause and listen to the inner voice from You before I act.

PSALMS 53:1 Only a fool would say to himself, "There is no God." And why does he say it? Because of his wicked heart, his dark and evil deeds. His life is corroded with sin.

THE NARWHAL

A relative of the beluga whale,
This creature of the sea.
His home is in the Arctic,
And his horn is a mystery.

The norwhal is sixteen feet in length,
With flippers small and round.
He survived the great whale slaughter
Because of where he's found.

The tusk may be up to nine feet long—
A straight and spiraled horn.
In years past, it was linked
To the fabled unicorn.

Narwhals are quite common in the Arctic. They live in small parties of up to fifty members, called "pods." Sometimes, however, they will combine to form huge herds of several thousand. The Eskimos use them for meat and blubber; their hide, known as muktuk, is prized as it remains supple when wet or frozen. They are also a good source of vitamin C. The male narwhal grows a long, twisted tusk, or horn, above the upper lip. It can be eight or nine feet long. Strangely enough, it almost always has a left-handed twist to it. Some people too have a strange twist in their outlook. They are reluctant to accept the existence of God. Oh, the price they will be required to pay!

Dear Heavenly Father, help me to effectively witness to others. When I fail to do so, I let You down. Teach me to be strong when I carry Your Word out into the world.

PROVERBS 22:1 If you must choose, take a good name rather than great riches, for to be held in loving esteem is better than silver or gold.

THE OCTOPUS

They call this creature "devilfish"
And think of him with fear,
And yet he is a shy one
And will quickly disappear.

He has no bones, so he can hide
In the smallest den.
When the way is clear,
He'll ooze right outside again.

His color changes easily
From yellow to red or brown.
He matches the surroundings
Where he happens to be found.

The octopus is a strange creature
With reputation rare—
He really doesn't deserve it,
But then, he really doesn't care!

There are many old sea stories told that malign the poor octopus—stories of huge octopi capsizing ships and wreaking havoc in the seas. This shy creature comes in a hundred-odd varieties, most of them from a fraction of an inch to three feet across. (There may be some bigger specimens in the depths of the Pacific, however.) The octopus suffers from a bad reputation. We must take heed and keep our own reputations spotless for we speak for the Lord. If we act in such a way as to sully our names, we are poor witnesses for Jesus Christ—and, unlike the octopus, we *do* care!

Dear Lord, I thank You for allowing me to be Your ambassador. I pray that I might be a good and true one and that the witness I give might lead others to You. When people speak my name, let it be with respect and love, not for myself, Lord, but for Your Spirit within me.

HEBREWS 10:22 Let us go right in, to God himself, with true hearts fully trusting him to receive us, because we have been sprinkled with Christ's blood to make us clean, and because our bodies have been washed with pure water.

THE PLATYPUS

The strange-looking platypus—
A mammal that lays eggs!
He's like a conglomeration
Of creatures on four legs.

He has a bill just like a duck
And a broad beaverlike tail.
He has webbed feet with which to swim,
And claws that can impale.

He grooms himself immaculately
And enjoys being clean.
The funny little platypus
Is very seldom seen.

The platypus weighs only two or three pounds and measures about twenty inches in length at most. It keeps itself clean and well-groomed, combing its long fur with its rear claws. It has a ball-and-socket joint in its rear hips and thus can reach its entire body. The platypus is a native of Australia, and its number is dwindling. Just as this strange animal keeps itself clean in the waters of the rivers, so do we keep ourselves clean spiritually in Jesus Christ. We have been cleansed of sin by Jesus' blood and by accepting and obeying His Word. Let us always keep our hearts clean and pure by applying His Word to our lives.

Dear Father, I pray that I may use Your Word to the fullest extent, keeping my life in good order as the platypus keeps its coat well-groomed and clean. Help me to be pure—outside and inside—that I might be a good witness for the Christian life.

I CORINTHIANS 3:13 There is going to come a time of testing at Christ's Judgment Day to see what kind of material each builder has used. Everyone's work will be put through the fire so that all can see whether or not it keeps its value, and what was really accomplished.

THE PRAIRIE DOG

Prairie dogs have disappeared
From where they used to be.
They used to build their prairie towns
Across the plains country.

Most of them are living now
In refuges and parks.
They still build their prairie towns,
But progress leaves its marks.

They work hard constructing their burrows,
And keep them in good repair.
When it comes to guarding from danger,
The whole population will share.

A prairie-dog town is fun to watch. There is so much activity! The black-tailed prairie dog is a plains animal while his cousin, the white-tail, lives in the mountains. The white-tail is less sociable than the black-tail. The plains prairie dog is quite a careful builder. It even builds a "listening post" close to the inside entrance of its tunnel. The entrance tunnel may be as long as sixteen feet and go almost straight down! What seems to be a large mound of dirt around the entrance is actually a circular dike, built to keep the water out. The burrow is carefully planned and executed.

Dear Lord, I pray that I may be as good at building my life as the prairie dog is at building its home. I have a firm foundation to build on, and I pray that my work will stand the testing that You promise.

PROVERBS 4:11,12 I would have you learn this great fact: that a life of doing right is the wisest life there is. If you live that kind of life, you'll not limp or stumble as you run.

THE RIGHT WHALE

How did the right whale
Get his name?
Because it was "right,"
And that's a shame.

It was the right whale
For whaling men—
Easy to catch,
And to float again.

A treasure of whalebone,
He was a prize!
He's now near extinction—
Men are using their eyes.

They watch for his spout
And his broad, black tail,
But they no longer kill
The gentle right whale.

You have heard the words, "being in the right place at the right time." It seems that the poor right whale was just the opposite. It was in the wrong place at the wrong time, and so it was almost destroyed because of its unwary attitude. It was so easy to catch and kill that it became a prime target of the whalers of old, who gave it its name. If we spend our lives doing right, being in the right places and doing the right things, we will not be an unwary target for the devil. He loves nothing more than to lure us to the wrong places, with the wrong companionship, that he might have the opportunity to drive the harpoon of sin deep into our hearts.

Dear Lord, teach me to be alert so I may be in the right place at the right time. Give me the strength to withstand the pull of wrong companions. Help me to realize that the devil is devious in his ways and will lull me into a false sense of security should I become lethargic. Let me take a lesson from the right whale, that I may be a right Christian for You!

I PETER 3:8 And now this word to all of you: You should be like one big happy family, full of sympathy toward each other, loving one another with tender hearts and humble minds.

THE SEA LION

"Mr. Show-off" he's been called
Because he loves to play.
He is a family man, you know,
And proves it day by day.

He maintains a harem of females,
And defends his family
From other males and predators,
Whoever they may be.

He has a mane of stiff, curled hair,
And though he doesn't roar,
He's often known to honk or bark
As he guards his strip of shore.

The sea lion enjoys its family and will fight viciously to protect each member of its "herd." As Christians, we are members of the family of God. We should show our concern for each other, and—like the sea lion—we should be ready to come to the aid of any member of the family at any time. Perhaps the circumstances will not be as dramatic as the sea lion's, but the response must be as swift. Maybe the best way to offer help is by providing a listening ear . . . a prayer . . . a word of encouragement or love. Or maybe something physical—food, clothing, or shelter. As we give, we grow in the Lord.

Dear Lord, teach me to keep my ears and eyes open to the needs of others. And please help me to open my heart and mind in answer to these needs. Let me be, as the sea lion patriarch, ready to defend and assist my Christian brothers and sisters in any way I can.

PROVERBS 24:5 A wise man is mightier than a strong man. Wisdom is mightier than strength.

THE SEA OTTER

The sea otter is known
For his coat of fur.
He once was sought by many,
And killed without a stir.

Men came to realize
Sea otters would disappear
If the hunting continued;
The fact became quite clear.

Now the fur-clad otters
Float upon the sea,
Feeding and enjoying
Life as it should be.

The adult sea otter is about four feet long, including the tail. It is a good swimmer, with powerful, webbed back feet. The forefeet are almost like hands, and the otter is often seen floating on its back, enjoying its dinner. Clasping a rock to break open shells, it uses its chest as a dinner table as it feasts on clams and other seafood. It is unique in that it uses tools (rocks) in this way. Thank goodness that we realized the danger of extinction before it was too late. Because the otters reproduce slowly, the danger was very real. Now that man is no longer a menace, their biggest worry is the shark, and they at least have a chance against that predator.

Dear Heavenly Father, I pray that I may use my "brain" instead of my "brawn." Help me to take the time to think before I act and to apply my knowledge to my actions. As we have hurt the poor sea otter without thought, so I may have hurt others. Forgive me, Lord, and help me to learn from past mistakes.

II CORINTHIANS 2:14,15 But thanks be to God! For through what Christ has done, he has triumphed over us so that now wherever we go he uses us to tell others about the Lord and to spread the Gospel like a sweet perfume. As far as God is concerned there is a sweet, wholesome fragrance in our lives. It is the fragrance of Christ within us, an aroma to both the saved and the unsaved all around us.

THE SKUNK

The skunk is a strange little creature,
A cousin to the civit cat.
His protection is a musky odor,
And there is nothing worse than that!

These animals teach a lesson—
They only come out at night,
And people must keep their distance
If they see a skunk in sight.

The smell chases off their enemies—
It even chases off their friends.
These small and lonely little creatures
Have to learn to stay downwind.

Just as the lowly skunk repels other creatures, including man, with its pungent, lingering odor, so we should be just the opposite. Truly, Christ is a sweet perfume, and as we are filled with His Spirit, we should attract others through our lives and attitudes. We have the best news known to man—the Good News of the Gospel—and if we let it work in our lives, it will overflow to those around us so they too might embrace the fragrance of Christ!

Dear Lord, help me to exude Your Glory and greatness. I pray that I might live my life to attract others to You and Your Way. Help me to always keep this in mind, that I might constantly grow in my Christian walk.

I PETER 5:7 Let him have all your worries and cares, for he is always thinking about you and watching everything that concerns you.

THE STICK INSECT

Stick insects look like sticks,
You'd hardly know they're there.
They blend with their surroundings,
And live most anywhere.

They do not like the winter cold,
And must escape or die.
They come in several colors,
And some of them can fly.

They can be motionless,
In a cataleptic state.
You can move their limbs around,
And they won't even break.

The stick insect is a member of the same order as the leaf insect. It is very sluggish, and since it resembles its surroundings so well, it is difficult to see. This inconspicuousness is its best defense against predators. It is truly dependent on God and fares well in nature's scheme of things. We too are dependent on the Lord. He will take our burdens of worry and care because He loves us. He is watching over us constantly, just as a loving father watches over his children. We are our Father's concern, and we can count on His teachings and His love. The stick insect blends in with its surroundings, and it is scarcely seen. Let us be set apart for Christ—out where we can be seen and counted. Let us be noted for our actions—the actions of true Christians, with love and concern for our fellow man.

Dear Lord, let me be a beacon for You! I pray that my life might reflect Your Light. Help me to play some little part in winning souls for Your Kingdom.

I PETER 3:4 Be beautiful inside, in your hearts, with the lasting charm of a gentle and quiet spirit which is so precious to God.

THE SWAN

*There is a legend that the swan
Sings before he dies.
A legend that has been proven true—
To many it's no surprise.*

*This beautiful creature, graceful and proud,
Starts out an ugly gray,
But grows into a beautiful bird
Of snowy white one day.*

*The long, arched neck and graceful glide
Upon the lake's blue calm
Have stirred artistic temperaments,
And provided the heart with balm.*

Yes, there is a calm and graceful beauty to the swan that is unforgettable once you have seen it. And as that beauty touches hearts, so should the beauty of Christ shine through us, helping us to win souls to Him. And as the swan sings a song upon dying, so should we, with a quiet joy in the knowledge of the promised eternity that lies ahead in Heaven with Him.

Dear Lord in Heaven, I pray that I may reflect the Holy Spirit in all that I do. Help me to radiate the "peace that passes all understanding" so that other souls might be led to You.

I JOHN 2:3 And how can we be sure that we belong to him? By looking within ourselves: are we really trying to do what he wants us to?

THE TIGER

The magnificent striped tiger
Stealthily stalks his prey—
Mighty, graceful giant,
Sleeping or romping in play.

He catnaps in the daytime
And hunts with falling night.
He may travel fifteen miles,
Before the prey's in sight.

He's a solitary creature,
And now his number's small.
Cunning, full of fluid grace—
The greatest cat of all!

The tiger is a magnificent animal! The beautiful pattern of its coat combines with the fluid grace of its movements to make it unexcelled in the animal kingdom. When we see it sleeping or romping in play, it is hard for us to realize that a killer instinct hides beneath that beautiful exterior. The tiger is a cunning hunter and stalks its prey from a distance, its huge, cushioned paws hardly making a sound. It kills only from need, not from greed. It performs its part in the cycle of nature.

Dear Father, help me to follow Your purpose in my life just as the mighty tiger follows the plan of nature. I pray that my motives might be pure and that I might be a witness to Your grace. I thank You for the opportunity to reflect Your Glory and the eternal Light of Life in Jesus.

MARK 3:24,25 A kingdom divided against itself will collapse. A home filled with strife and division destroys itself.

THE WOLF

We list the wolves as "endangered."
Their numbers now are few.
They really have fewer enemies,
Than other animals do.

They are affectionate and loyal
Within the family realm,
And in their social order,
The parents are at the helm.

All the family members
Share responsibility
Of caring for the young ones,
So the mother can be free.

Free to help with hunting,
And not be so confined.
They live together in a group,
In love and peace of mind.

When wolves hunt, they hunt the ill, the young, or the very old of the prey, so actually they keep the prey herds healthy. Wolves are curious creatures and may circle a man just to investigate, not to attack. They can weigh from sixty to a hundred twenty pounds and can be dangerous when hungry or excited. They run in a pack, and that pack is usually a family unit. The parents are ordinarily the pack leaders, and they patrol territorial boundaries, settle disputes, and control the movements of the pack. Much loyal affection is shown between the family members.

Dear Father in Heaven, help us, Your children, to listen to Your teachings and follow Your ways as the wolf pack follows its leader. I pray that we may work together in Your Name for the alliance that peace requires.

Bibliography

CHRISTIAN CONTENT

The following is a partial list of some of my favorite Christian books—I wish I could list them all! Of course it goes without saying that the greatest textbook of all is God's Own Word, the Bible.

Borland, Hal. *Hill Country Harvest*. New York: J.B. Lippencott, 1976. A folksy, and informative book that warrants the time to read and enjoy. The author has much to convey about the surrounding New England countryside and God's creatures who share it.

Castagno, Anthony J., with Faye C. Allen and Joseph M. Castagno. *A Treasury of Biblical Quotations*. Nashville: Thomas Nelson Publishers, 1980. A topical anthology of Scripture quotations. This has been a great help to me.

Christenson, Evelyn. *"Lord, Change Me!"*. Wheaton, Illinois: Victor Books, 1977.

Getz, Gene A. *Building Up One Another*. Wheaton, Illinois: Victor Books, 1976.

Marshall, Catherine. *Beyond Ourselves*. New York: McGraw-Hill, 1961.

Pinson, William. *The Word Topical Bible of Issues and Answers*. Carmel, N.Y.: Word, Inc., 1981.

Price, Eugeia. *The Wider Place*. Grand Rapids, Mich.: Zondervan Publishers, 1966. A beautiful book, one of my all-time favorites.

Rogers, Adrian. *The Secret of Supernatural Living*. Nashville: Thomas Nelson Publishers, 1982. An uplifting book on the presence of God's Spirit in you.

Smith, Anna Whithall. *The Christian's Secret of a Happy Life*. Old Tappan, N.J.: Fleming H. Revell, Co., first printed in 1870. It may be an old book, but the content is as contemporary as today. A must for every Christian.

Souter, John C. *Growing Stronger*. Wheaton, Illinois: Tyndale House Publishers, 1980. Basically a study book to bring the reader closer to the Scriptures and to aid in spiritual growth. A real "thinking" book.

NATURE CONTENT

Cansdale, G.S. *All the Animals of the Bible Lands.* Grand Rapids, Mi.: Zondervan Publishing, 1970.

Birds: Their Life, Their Ways, Their World, Pleasantville, N.Y.: The Reader's Digest Association, Inc., 1979.

Cavendish, Marshall. *Encyclopedia of Animal Life.* New York: Marshall Cavendish Ltd., 1973. Also published as the *International Wildlife Encyclopedia.* This is a marvelous learning and reference tool with full-color illustrations and easy-to-read information for the professional and layman alike.

Hopf, Alice L. *Misunderstood Animals.* New York: McGraw-Hill, 1973.

Lemmon, Robert S. *All About Strange Beasts of the Present.* New York: Random House, 1957. A good book for the young animal-lover.

Marvels and Mysteries of Our Animal World. Pleasantville, N.Y.: The Reader's Digest Association, Inc., 1964.

Our Magnificent Wildlife: How to Enjoy and Preserve It. Pleasantville, N.Y.: The Reader's Digest Association, Inc., 1975.

Paulsen, Gary. *The Small Ones—Real Animals.* Milwaukee: Raintree Editions, 1976. This is an utterly charming and informative book on rabbits, mice, and foxes. It is well-illustrated with pictures and photographs. Good for any age, written in an easy and captivating style.

Peterson, Roger Tory. *A Field Guide to the Birds.* Cambridge: The Riverside Press, 1980.

Roots, Clive. *Animals of the Dark.* New York: Praeger Publishers, 1974.

Schaefer, Jack. *An American Bestiary.* Boston: Houghton-Mifflin, Co., 1975.

Tee-Van, Helen Damrosch. *Insects Are Where You Find Them.* New York: Alfred A. Knopf, 1963.

The World Encyclopedia of Animals. Mountain View, Ca.: World Publishing Co., 1972.

Tweedie, Michael. *Insect Life.* London: Collins, 1977.

Subject Index

Amphibians

Arrow-poison frog, 120
Axolotl, 68
Fire-bellied toad, 193
Horned frog, 166
Natterjack toad, 30

Birds

Albatross, 127
Apostlebird, 51
Bald eagle, 4
Bellbird, 6
Bird of paradise, 69
Buzzard, 187
Cardinal, 85
Cormorant, 86
Crow, 191
Dodo bird, 72
Dove, 132
Flamingo, 159
Goose, 14
Hammerhead, 199
Heron, 17
Honey Guide, 135
Hoopoe, 18
Hornbill, 19
Hummingbird, 91
Jacana, 22
Kingfisher, 204
Kittiwake, 205
Kiwi bird, 136
Limpkin, 27
Loon, 116
Lovebird, 59
Lyrebird, 208
Martin, 61
Mockingbird, 139
Nightingale, 118
Osprey, 33
Ostrich, 34
Owl, 78
Oxpecker, 62
Palm dove, 120
Parrot, 172
Peacock, 121
Pelican, 35
Penguin, 144
Phalarope, 36
Pied wagtail, 94
Roadrunner, 42
Robin, 43
Scrubbird, 122

Sea gull, 97
Shrike, 174
Stilt, 45
Stone curlew, 99
Stork, 46
Storm petrel, 150
Swan, 220
Tailorbird, 47
Woodpecker, 179

Fish

Archerfish, 67
Barracuda, 104
Bitterling, 106
Boxfish, 186
Climbing perch, 157
Clownfish, 9
Four-eyed fish, 89
Garpike, 195
Glassfish, 197
Hatchet fish, 15
Ice fish, 113
Jawfish, 114
Leaf fish, 206
Ling, 28
Lumpsucker, 207
Mudskipper, 141
Oarfish, 76
Ocean sunfish, 142
Pilot fish, 38
Salmon, 147
Sea horse, 79
Stingray, 175

Insects

Ant, 83
Butterfly, 70
Click beetle, 8
Cockroach, 190
Cricket, 109
Dragonfly, 158
Firefly, 133
Grasshopper, 162
Green lacewing, 163
Honey ant, 56
Honey bee, 57
Harvester, 164
Hornet, 74
Housefly, 167
Ladybird beetle, 92
Orb spider, 119
Praying mantis, 64

Spider, 80
Stick insect, 219

Mammals

Aardvark, 183
Addax, 82
Armadillo, 184
Aye-aye, 3
Baboon, 154
Bat, 185
Bear, 155
Beaver, 84
Bison, 105
Blue whale, 52
Camel, 129
Canadian lynx, 171
Caribou, 188
Chevrotain, 107
Chimpanzee, 131
Chipmunk, 108
Deer, 11
Dormouse, 12
Douroucouli, 192
Elephant, 53
Elephant shrew, 88
Field mouse, 13
Fox, 134
Galago, 160
Gerenuk, 196
Giant panda, 161
Gibbon, 110
Giraffe, 54
Gray squirrel, 90
Harvest mouse, 201
Hedgehog, 111
Hippopotamus, 165
Hyena, 168
Hyrax, 112
Indri, 21
Jaguarundi, 23
Joey, 24
Kangaroo, 169
Klipspringer, 25
Koala bear, 115
Leopard, 58
Lion, 138
Long-eared jerboa, 75
Manatee, 209
Mole, 210
Mountain goat, 29
Muskrat, 93
Narwhal, 211

North American pika, 31
Ocelot, 77
Opossum, 32
Pack rat, 171
Platypus, 213
Pilot whale, 39
Pocket gopher, 95
Porcupine, 40
Porpoise, 63
Prairie dog, 214
Rabbit, 145
Raccoon, 96
Rhinocerous, 41
Right whale, 215
Sea lion, 216
Sea otter, 217
Skunk, 218
Sloth, 98
Stoat, 176
Suricate, 123
Tahr, 177
Tiger, 221
Warthog, 124
Wolf, 222
Woodchuck, 48
Zebra, 180

Mollusks and Echinoderms

Abalone, 103
Centipede, 156
Chambered nautilus, 7
Hermit crab, 16
Jellyfish, 202
Octopus, 212
Oyster, 143
Sea anenome, 148
Snail, 149
Starfish, 44

Reptiles

Alligator, 153
Basilisk lizard, 5
Chameleon, 130
Chuckwalla, 189
Frilled lizard, 194
Gecko lizard, 73
Green turtle, 198
Komodo dragon, 170
Leathery turtle, 137
Moloch lizard, 117
Rattlesnake, 173

Scripture Index

Acts
2:33, 6
4:32, 51
20:35, 56

Amos
4:13, 35

Colossians
1:11,12, 130
3:11, 176
3:17, 193

I Corinthians
3:13, 214
12:1, 73
12:4,5, 72
12:27, 78
13:7, 59
13:11,12a, 68
15:58, 91
16:13, 89

II Corinthians
2:14,15, 218
4:8,9, 44
4:17,18, 143
5:17, 70
12:10b, 38

Daniel
2:20, 107

Deuteronomy
31:8, 32
32:11, 4
33:27a, 47

Ecclesiastes
5:19b,20, 61
7:14, 127

Ephesians
2:13, 24
3:20, 81
4:11, 77
5:1, 206
5:19, 144
6:5,8, 86
6:11,13, 19

Ezekiel
33:4,5, 186

Galatians
1:8, 192
5:13, 92
5:25,26, 177
6:4,5, 120
6:9, 139
6:14, 119

Genesis
1:21,26, 209
1:31a, 198

Hebrews
3:14, 141
4:13, 197
4:14, 123
10:22, 213
10:24, 62
10:36, 131
12:2, 17
12:15b, 156

Isaiah
11:3,4a, 54
29:15, 190
30:21, 185
66:1,2, 114

James
1:5,8, 36
1:14,16, 148
1:21, 105
2:12,13, 162
3:5, 179
3:10,12, 174
4:17, 97
5:16, 191

Jeremiah
8:7a, 46

Job
12:10,11, 21

I John
1:7, 113
2:3, 221
2:29, 106
4:18,19, 30

John
3:16, 7
4:10, 117
4:34, 136
5:28,29, 15
7:37b,38, 129
10:14,15, 104
12:37, 204
13:34,35, 58

Luke
6:39b, 39
10:2, 201
12:25,26, 27

Mark
3:24,25, 222
8:36,37, 171
13:35-37, 99
16:15,16, 194

Matthew
4:5-7, 205
5:15,16, 133
5:21,22a, 182
6:22,23, 160
6:31-33, 16
6:34, 48
7:21, 76
7:24-27, 199
13:20,21, 82
14:29b,30, 5
28:19,20a, 187

I Peter
2:1-3a, 159
2:15, 85
3:4, 220
3:8, 216
5:7, 219

Proverbs

3:6, *67*
3:21-23, *134*
4:7, *173*
4:11,12, *215*
6:6, *83*
10:4, *96*
10:26, *98*
11:13, *172*
12:21, *12*
13:3, *166*
13:16, *95*
13:20, *167*
14:26, *11*
15:28, *212*
16:24, *57*
16:26, *11*
15:28, *210*
16:24, *57*
16:26,27, *88*
16:32, *165*
17:14, *154*
17:17, *52*
18:17, *157*
18:24, *63*
20:6, *94*
20:7, *22*
20:11, *153*
20:27, *135*
21:20, *90*
22:1, *212*
22:3, *79*
22:6, *53*
22:17-19, *75*
24:3,4, *74*
24:5, *217*
24:13,14, *155*
25:18, *175*
25:19, *207*
26:27, *64*
27:7, *170*
27:12, *93*
28:1, *138*
29:8, *161*
29:23, *69*
29:25, *40*
31:30, *163*

Psalms

4:1, *189*
5:3, *116*
5:8, *147*
5:11,12, *120*
7:10, *31*
9:1,2, *121*
13:5, *41*
18:33, *29*
19:7-11, *111*
24:1, *171*
25:4,5, *42*
30:4,5, *137*
32:8, *45*
33:1, *118*
48:14, *14*
51:10, *164*
53:1, *211*
54:4, *9*
55:6-8, *132*
66:1,2, *109*
67:2,3, *208*
86:11, *80*
89:1,2, *18*
94:8-10, *168*
95:6,7, *124*
104:24, *13*
107:28-30, *150*
108:1, *108*
108:2-5, *110*
109:21, *23*
119:1-3, *43*
119:73, *183*
136:23,24, *8*
139:13,14, *112*
146:6,7, *115*
147:1, *122*
148:7, *103*

Revelation

2:10b, *33*

Romans

6:23, *3*
8:5, *158*
8:38,39, *149*
13:12,13a, *184*
15:4, *196*
15:5, *169*

Samuel

22:2,3, *28*
22:36, *142*
22:47, *34*

Timothy

2:19, *25*
2:25, *188*
4:6-8, *202*

Titus

2:7, *195*

I Thessalonians

4:11,12a, *145*

II Thessalonians

3:10, *84*